What Readers Are Saying About
The Passionate Programmer

If you are passionate about software craftsmanship, if you want to be a great software developer, if you want to love your work, or if you want to raise the bar and turn software development into a *profession* instead of a job, then read this book. In these pages, Chad Fowler presents a set of no-nonsense heuristics, disciplines, and attitudes that will teach you how to respect and love your profession—and be great at it.

➤ **Bob Martin**
   President, Object Mentor, Inc.

The great thing about this book is that it is full of plans—things I can do. It keeps responsibility for my situation where it belongs—on me. This book makes it clear that I'm not alone, it shows that my situation is not uniquely scary, and it explains what I can do today. And tomorrow. And for the rest of my career.

➤ **Kent Beck**
   Programmer

Six short months before I read Chad's book, I was on the verge of changing careers. Through a series of accidents from November to May, I decided not only to stick with software development but to be passionate about it while striving to be *great*. With a healthy dose of inspiration, the book you're now holding served as a road map for achieving those goals.

➤ **Sammy Larbi**
   Chief Spaghetti Coder, codeodor.com

The Passionate Programmer

Creating a Remarkable Career
in Software Development

Chad Fowler

The Pragmatic Bookshelf

Dallas, Texas • Raleigh, North Carolina

Many of the designations used by manufacturers and sellers to distinguish their products are claimed as trademarks. Where those designations appear in this book, and The Pragmatic Programmers, LLC was aware of a trademark claim, the designations have been printed in initial capital letters or in all capitals. The Pragmatic Starter Kit, The Pragmatic Programmer, Pragmatic Programming, Pragmatic Bookshelf, PragProg and the linking *g* device are trademarks of The Pragmatic Programmers, LLC.

Every precaution was taken in the preparation of this book. However, the publisher assumes no responsibility for errors or omissions, or for damages that may result from the use of information (including program listings) contained herein.

Our Pragmatic courses, workshops, and other products can help you and your team create better software and have more fun. For more information, as well as the latest Pragmatic titles, please visit us at *http://pragprog.com*.

Printed in the United States of America.

ISBN-13: 978-1-934356-34-0

Printed on acid-free paper.

Book version: P7.0—November 2013

For Kelly Jeanne

Contents

Foreword xi

Acknowledgments xiii

Introduction xv

Part I — Choosing Your Market

Tip 1. Lead or Bleed?   5
Tip 2. Supply and Demand   9
Tip 3. Coding Don't Cut It Anymore   13
Tip 4. Be the Worst   16
Tip 5. Invest in Your Intelligence   19
Tip 6. Don't Listen to Your Parents   22
Tip 7. Be a Generalist   27
Tip 8. Be a Specialist   32
Tip 9. Don't Put All Your Eggs in Someone Else's Basket   35
Tip 10. Love It or Leave It   37

Part II — Investing in Your Product

Tip 11. Learn to Fish   47
Tip 12. Learn How Businesses Really Work   50
Tip 13. Find a Mentor   52
Tip 14. Be a Mentor   56
Tip 15. Practice, Practice, Practice   59
Tip 16. The Way That You Do It   64
Tip 17. On the Shoulders of Giants   67
Tip 18. Automate Yourself into a Job   70

Part III — Executing

Tip 19. Right Now   81
Tip 20. Mind Reader   83
Tip 21. Daily Hit   86
Tip 22. Remember Who You Work For   89
Tip 23. Be Where You're At   92
Tip 24. How Good a Job Can I Do Today?   95
Tip 25. How Much Are You Worth?   98
Tip 26. A Pebble in a Bucket of Water   101
Tip 27. Learn to Love Maintenance   104
Tip 28. Eight-Hour Burn   108
Tip 29. Learn How to Fail   111
Tip 30. Say "No"   114
Tip 31. Don't Panic   117
Tip 32. Say It, Do It, Show It   121

Part IV — Marketing... Not Just for Suits

Tip 33. Perceptions, Perschmeptions   133
Tip 34. Adventure Tour Guide   136
Tip 35. Me Rite Reel Nice   139
Tip 36. Being Present   141
Tip 37. Suit Speak   145
Tip 38. Change the World   147
Tip 39. Let Your Voice Be Heard   149
Tip 40. Build Your Brand   153
Tip 41. Release Your Code   155
Tip 42. Remarkability   158
Tip 43. Making the Hang   161

Part V — Maintaining Your Edge

Tip 44. Already Obsolete   170
Tip 45. You've Already Lost Your Job   173
Tip 46. Path with No Destination   175
Tip 47. Make Yourself a Map   177
Tip 48. Watch the Market   179
Tip 49. That Fat Man in the Mirror   181
Tip 50. The South Indian Monkey Trap   184
Tip 51. Avoid Waterfall Career Planning   188

Tip 52. Better Than Yesterday   191
Tip 53. Go Independent   195
    Have Fun **199**

    Resources **201**

Foreword

I believe that everyone has remarkable in them but that it takes finding something they truly care about to draw it out. You can't be remarkable if you don't love your environment, your tools, and your domain.

Before I had my spark lit with 37signals and Ruby on Rails, I went through a series of jobs and gigs that certainly wouldn't fit the bill as remarkable. I was treading water and just letting one day eat the next. Before I knew it, six months were gone, and I didn't have anything to show for it.

That's a terrible feeling of regret. I hate the feeling that my presence doesn't really matter and that the world would have been exactly no different in a meaningful way if my work hadn't been done. To become remarkable, you have to believe that you're making a significant dent in the universe.

When I wasn't making a dent at work, it spilled over to my personal life too. When I didn't feel like I was having an impact during office hours, it was that much harder to muster the effort to have an impact afterward.

To me, leading a remarkable career is the best way I know to kick start that same desire for leading a remarkable life—one where you don't just become a better and more valuable worker, but you become a better human too.

That's why this book is so important. It's not just about making better widgets and feeling secure in your job. It's just as much about developing the skills and sensibilities for leading a more rewarding life filled with many remarkable aspects, with work just being one of them.

—David Heinemeier Hansson
Creator of Ruby on Rails and partner in 37signals

Acknowledgments

I would have never written a book if not for Dave Thomas and Andy Hunt. *The Pragmatic Programmer: From Journeyman to Master* [HT00] served as a catalyst for me, and I've been inspired by their work ever since. Without Dave's encouragement and guidance, I would have never believed I was qualified to write this.

Susannah Pfalzer edited the second edition of the book. By "edited," I mean pushed, inspired, championed, drove, and of course...edited. Her patience and ability to say just the right thing to get me motivated without scaring me into hiding were exactly what I needed to get the book done. If not for Susannah, the book would still be a messy collection of rambling half-formed ideas.

David Heinemeier Hansson contributed the foreword. His career as partner in 37signals and the creator of Rails is a shining example of the ideas laid out in this book. I was also lucky enough to get contributions from some of the remarkable people I've met along the way in my career. Huge thanks to Stephen Akers, James Duncan Davidson, Vik Chadha, Mike Clark, Patrick Collison, and Tom Preston-Werner for inspiring me and my book's readers.

A number of reviewers provided excellent feedback on drafts of the second edition. It's always surprising how wrong the first version of a chapter can be and how right a good reviewer can make it. Thanks to Sammy Larbi, Bryan Dyck, Bob Martin, Kent Beck, Alan Francis, Jared Richardson, Rich Downie, and Erik Kastner.

Juliet Thomas served as an editor early in the process of writing the first edition of this book. Her enthusiasm and perspective were invaluable. I received an amazing amount of feedback from first-edition reviewers: Carey Boaz, Karl Brophey, Brandon Campbell, Vik Chadha, Mauro Cicio, Mark Donoghue, Pat Eyler, Ben Goodwin, Jacob Harris, Adam Keys, Steve Morris, Bill Nall, Wesley Reiz, Avik Sengupta, Kent Spillner, Sandesh Tattitali, Craig Utley, Greg Vaughn, and Peter W. A. Wood. They truly made the book better, and I can't thank them enough for their time, energy, and insight.

The ideas in this book were inspired by the many great people I've had the opportunity to work with, both officially and unofficially, over the years. For listening, teaching, and talking, thanks to Donnie Webb, Ken Smith, Walter Hoehn, James McMurry, Carey Boaz, David Alan Black, Mike Clark, Nicole Clark, Vik Chadha, Avi Bryant, Rich Kilmer, Steve Akers, Mark Gardener, Ryan Ownens, Tom Copeland, Dave Craine, John Athayde, Marcel Molina, Erik Kastner, Bruce Williams, David Heinemeier Hansson, Ali Sareea, and Jim Weirich.

Thanks to my parents for their constant support. And most important, thanks go to my wife, Kelly, for making this all worthwhile.

Introduction

This book is about finding fulfillment and happiness in your career. Fulfillment and happiness don't (often) come by chance. They require thought, intention, action, and a willingness to change course when you've made mistakes. This book lays out a strategy for planning and creating a radically successful career (and, therefore, life) in software development.

The book is also about cultivating the desire to live a remarkable life. Strangely, we don't all set out on the quest to lead remarkable lives when we start our careers. Most of us are content to go with the flow. Our expectations have been lowered for us by the media and by our friends, acquaintances, and family members. So, leading a remarkable life is something you have to discover as even being a reasonable goal. It's not obvious.

Most people spend far more of their waking adulthood working than doing anything else. According to a 2006 survey by the U.S. Bureau of Labor Statistics,[1] average Americans spend half of their waking time at work. Leisure and sports are a distant 15 percent of waking time spent. The facts show that our lives basically *are* our work.

If your life is primarily consumed by your work, then loving your work is one of the most important keys to loving your *life*. Challenging, motivating, rewarding work is more likely to make you want to get up in the morning than dull, average tasks. Doing your job well means that the activity you do for 50 percent of your available time is something you're good at. Conversely, if you don't do your job well, a large amount of your time will be spent feeling inadequate or guilty over not performing at your best.

Ultimately, we're all looking for happiness. Once we have our basic human needs like food and shelter taken care of, most of our goals

---

1.   http://www.bls.gov/tus/charts/

are geared toward finding happiness. Sadly, our *activities* are often mismatched to that one overarching goal. This is because we as humans get bogged down in the means and forget about the end.

I might be happier if I had more money. I might be happier if I got more and better recognition for my accomplishments. I might be happier if I were promoted in my company or I became famous. But what if I were poor and had a trivial job but I was really happy? Is that possible? If it were, should I be looking for more money? Or a better job?

Maybe not. What's certain is that, with the focused goal of happiness as a primary motivator, we can make better decisions about the smaller steps we take to achieve that goal. A higher salary might actually be desirable and lead toward happiness. But if you take your eyes off the primary goal, you can find yourself driving toward a higher salary at the *expense* of your happiness. It sounds ridiculous, but I've done it. And so have you. Think about it.

Throughout this book, I'm going to give you advice that I hope will lead you to a happier and more rewarding career (and thereby to a happier life). You might make more money if you follow this advice. You might gain more recognition or even become famous. But please don't forget that these are not the goals. They're a means to an end.

Failure Is Off the Radar!

One of the major steps along the road to creating a remarkable career for myself was, ironically, writing the first edition of this book. The book used to be called *My Job Went to India (And All I Got Was This Lousy Book): 52 Ways to Save Your Job*. It had a picture on the cover of a guy holding a sign that said "Will Code for Food." It was funny, and its title and shocking red cover were meant to play on the Western world's fears that their jobs were going to be outsourced to low-cost offshore programming teams.

The problem, though, is that it painted the wrong picture. The truth of the matter is, if you need to "save" your job, I can't help you. This book isn't about struggling to maintain the level of mediocrity required not to get fired. It's about being *awesome*. It's about *winning*. You don't win a race by trying not to lose. And you don't win at life by trying not to suck. Fortunately, the content of the book has never been about trying not to suck. I can't think that way, and neither should you.

I remember the exact moment when I decided that my career would be remarkable. I'd been coasting through jobs sort of how I coasted through high school, the part of college I finished, and my brief and somewhat mediocre career as a professional saxophonist. Because of some combination of luck and natural talent, I managed to come across a healthy amount of success along the way—enough that it landed me a well-paying job as a respected member of the technical staff of one of the world's "most admired" companies. But I was just *getting by*, and I knew it.

One evening after work, while browsing through the local bookstore, I came across Kent Beck's *Extreme Programming Explained: Embrace Change* [Bec00] on the new releases shelf. The subtitle of the book was *Embrace Change*. The idea of change has always been appealing to me. I have a tiny attention span that had, up until that point, manifested itself as a series of fast job changes—hopping from one company to the next. The idea of a "software development methodology" sounded atrociously boring and management-tinged, but I figured if it involved lots of change, it might be something I could push at work to avoid getting bored and feeling like I needed to find a new job.

Picking up this book turned out to be a really lucky whim. I started reading the book, and I couldn't put it down. After devouring its content, I hit the Internet and read everything I could about the ideas of Extreme Programming (XP). I was sufficiently moved by those ideas that I went to our chief information officer and attempted to sell him on the idea. He and his staff were convinced, and as part of the Extreme Programming adoption deal, he sent a large group of us to Object Mentor's Extreme Programming Immersion course.

Extreme Programming Immersion was *the* place to go if you wanted to learn about XP. It was like getting a backstage pass to a weeklong concert put on by our favorite rock stars. Being in that room with those people actually made me a *lot* smarter. It made me more creative. And, when it was over, I was really, really sad. I couldn't imagine going back to my cubicle and beating my head against the mediocrity I had grown accustomed to at work.

My co-worker Steve, who contributed the essay you'll find *Can't We Just....*, on page 164, and I came to the same conclusion. The only way to find yourself around *those* people as often as possible is to *become* one of those people. In other words, if I wanted to be around people who brought me up a level or two when I interacted with them, there wasn't a company I could apply to work at or a college course I could sign up for. I just had to identify what it meant to be one of those people and do what it took. So, I announced to Steve that I was going to become one of those people.

That was *the* turning point of my career. I somehow forgot it until years later when Steve reminded me of the conversation. I had told him about the fact that I had, for the first time, been invited to give a keynote speech at a conference. I was blown away that anyone would ask *me* of all people to not only speak but to deliver one of the main addresses to a software conference. I had indeed become one of those people I had aspired to become.

I did all of this without a formal education in computer programming. I was a musician before becoming a computer programmer. I went to college to study music. Since musicians don't benefit much from college degrees, I chose to avoid any class that didn't help me be a better musician. This means I left the university with more credits than required for any degree but still a few years worth of actual class time before I could graduate. In that way, I'm unqualified to be a professional software developer—at least if you look at the typical requirements for a software engineering position on the job market.

But, though I'm unqualified to be a typical software developer, my background as a musician gave me one key insight that ultimately allowed me to skip the step of being a typical software developer (who wants to be typical, anyway?). *Nobody* becomes a musician because they want to get a job and lead a stable and comfortable life. The music industry is too cruel an environment for this to be a feasible plan. People who become professional musicians *all* want to be *great*. At least when starting out, greatness is binary in the music world. A musician wants to either be great (and famous for it!) or not do it at all.

I'm often asked why it is that there are so many good musicians who are also good software developers. That's the reason. It's not because the brain functions are the same or that they're both detail-oriented or both require creativity. It's because a person who wants to be great is *far* more likely to become great than someone who just wants to do their job. And even if we can't all be Martin Fowler, Linus

Torvalds, or the Pragmatic Programmers, setting a high target makes it likely that we'll at least land somewhere far above average.

You Own It

Most people follow everyone else's plan but their own. To start differentiating yourself, all you have to do is stop and take a good look at your career. You need to be following *your* plan for you—not theirs.

How do you come up with this plan? Software is a business. As software developers, we are businesspeople. Our companies don't employ us because they love us. They never have, and they never will. That's not the job of a business. Businesses don't exist so we can have a place to go every day. The purpose of a business is to make money. To excel at a company, you're going to have to understand how you fit into the business's plan to make money.

As we'll explore later, keeping you employed costs your company a significant amount of money. Your company is *investing* in you. Your challenge is to become an obviously good investment. You will start to judge your own performance in terms of the business value you bring to the organization or customer who is employing you.

Think of your career as if it is the life cycle of a product that you are creating. That product is made up of you and your skills. In this book, we'll look at four facets that a business must focus on when designing, manufacturing, and selling a product. And we'll see how these four facets can be applied to our careers:

- *Choose your market.* Pick the technologies and the business domains you focus on consciously and deliberately. How do you balance risk and reward? How do supply and demand factor into the decision?

- *Invest in your product.* Your knowledge and skills are the cornerstone of your product. Properly investing in them is a critical part of making yourself marketable. Simply knowing how to program in Visual Basic or Java isn't good enough anymore. What other skills might you need in the new economy?

- *Execute.* Simply having employees with a strong set of skills does not pay off for a company. The employees have to *deliver*. How do you keep up the delivery pace without driving yourself into the dirt? How do you know you're delivering the *right* value for the company?

- *Market!* The best product in history will not get purchased if nobody knows it exists. How do you get find recognition in both your company and the industry as a whole without "sucking up"?

New Edition

This book is a second edition of the book originally titled *My Job Went to India (And All I Got Was This Lousy Book): 52 Ways to Save Your Job*. The goal of the second edition was to focus more closely on what the original book's real intent was: to create a remarkable career. In doing so, I not only created a new, more positive title, but I added new content as well.

David Heinemeir Hansson, the creator of Ruby on Rails and partner in 37signals, contributed a new foreword.

Each section contains one or more essays written by people I've encountered or worked with whose careers are truly remarkable. The essays provide insights into the decisions these innovators, developers, managers, and entrepreneurs have made along their paths to success. They also underscore the fact that the techniques outlined here aren't just idealistic suggestions applicable only in a perfect environment. They're real things that real people can do and accomplish.

Some of the original tips have been removed, and several new tips have been added. The entire last section from the original, called "If You Can't Beat 'Em" was removed. New tips were added throughout the book that reflect new lessons I've learned since the first edition was published.

Some new "Act on It" sections have been added to tips held over from the previous edition.

This introduction and the ending have been replaced to reflect the book's clearer focus on the goal of a remarkable career.

The goal of this book is to give you a systematic way of building a remarkable career in software development. We will walk through specific examples and present a set of actions that you can take *right now* that will have both short-term and long-term positive effects.

And, like I said before, we're not going to talk about how to save your job. If you currently find yourself feeling afraid about losing your job, the steps you'll take to build a remarkable career will remove that fear. Remarkable software developers don't languish. They don't find themselves fruitlessly searching for work. So, don't worry. Stay focused on winning, and the fear of losing will be forever a memory.

Part I

Choosing Your Market

You're about to make a *big* investment. It may not be a lot of money, but it's your time—your life. Many of us just float down the stream of our careers, letting the current take us where it may. We just happen to get into Java or Visual Basic, and then our employers finally spring for a training class on one of the latest industry buzzwords. So, we float down that path for a while until something else is handed to us. Our career is one big series of undirected coincidences.

In *The Pragmatic Programmer: From Journeyman to Master* [HT00], Dave Thomas and Andy Hunt talk about *programming by coincidence*. Most programmers can relate to the idea: you start working on something, add a little code here, and add a little more there. Maybe you start with an example program that you copy and paste from a website. It seems to work, so you change it a little to be more like the program you really need. You don't really understand what you're doing, but you keep nudging the program around until it almost completely meets your needs. The trouble is, you don't understand how it works, and like a house of cards, each new feature you add increases the likelihood your program will fall apart.

As a software developer, it's pretty obvious that programming by coincidence is a bad thing. Yet so many of us allow important career choices to be, in effect, coincidences. Which technologies should we invest in? Which domain should we develop expertise in? Should we go broad or deep with our knowledge? These are questions we really should be asking ourselves.

Imagine you've started a company and you're developing what is destined to be the company's flagship product. Without a "hit" with this product, your company is going to go bankrupt. How much attention do you pay to who your target customers are? Before actually manufacturing the product, how much thought do you put into what the product actually *is*? None of us would let decisions like these be made for us. We'd be completely attentive to every detail of the decision-making process.

So, why is it that most of us don't pay this kind of attention to the choices we make in our careers? If you think of your career as a business (which it *is*), your "product" is made up of the services you have to offer.

What are those services? Who are you going to sell them to? Is demand for your services going to grow or decline over the coming years? How big of a gamble are you willing to take on these choices?

This part of the book will help you answer these important questions for yourself.

Lead or Bleed?

If you're going to invest your money, a lot of options are available to you. You could put it in a savings account, but the interest it accrues probably wouldn't keep up with the pace of inflation. You could put it in government savings bonds. Again, you don't make much money as a result, but they're safe bets.

Or, you could invest your money in a small startup company. You may, for example, put up several thousand dollars in exchange for a small portion of ownership in the company. If the company's idea is good and it's able to execute effectively on that idea, you could potentially make a *lot* of money. On the other hand, you have no guarantee that you'll even recoup your original investment.

This concept is nothing new. You start to learn it as a child playing games. *If I run straight down the middle, it might surprise everyone, and nobody will tag me.* You are reminded of it constantly throughout daily life. You make the risk-reward trade-off when you're late for a meeting and trying to decide on the right route to work. *If traffic isn't bad, I can get there 15 minutes quicker if I drive down 32nd Street. If traffic is bad, I'm toast.*

The risk-reward trade-off is an important part of making intentional choices about which technologies and domains to invest in. Fifteen years ago, a very low-risk choice would have been to learn how to program in COBOL. Of course, there were also so many COBOL programmers to compete with that the average salary of a COBOL programmer at the time was not phenomenal. You could easily have found work, but the work wouldn't have been especially lucrative. Low risk. Low reward.

On the other hand, if at the same time you had chosen to investigate the new Java language from Sun Microsystems, it might have been difficult to find employment at a company that was actually doing anything with Java for a while. Who knew if anyone would *eventually* do anything with Java?

But, if you were looking at the state of the industry at that time, as Sun was, you may have seen something special in Java. You may have had a strong feeling that it was going to be big. Investing in it early would make you a leader in a big, upcoming technology trend.

Of course, in that instance, you would have been correct. And, if you played your cards right, your personal investment in Java may have been a very lucrative one. High risk. High reward.

Now imagine that, also 15 years ago, you saw a demonstration of the new BeOS from Be. It was incredible at the time. It was built from the ground up to take advantage of multiple processors. The multimedia capabilities were simply astounding. The platform created a definite buzz, and the pundits were giddy in anticipation of a solid new contender on the operating system block. With the new platform, of course, came new ways of programming, new APIs, and new user interface concepts. It was a lot to learn, but it may have really seemed worth it. You could have poured a lot of effort into becoming the first person to create, for example, an FTP client or a personal information manager for the BeOS. As Be released an Intel-compatible version of its operating system, rumors circulated about Apple buying the company out to use its technology as the foundation for the next generation of the Macintosh operating system.

Apple didn't buy Be. And, eventually, it became clear that Be wasn't going to capture even a niche market. The product just didn't stick. Many developers who had mastered programming for the BeOS environment became slowly and painfully aware that their investment was not going to pay off in the long-term. Eventually, Be was purchased by Palm, and the operating system was discontinued. BeOS was a risky but attractive technology investment that didn't yield concrete long-term returns for the developers who chose to invest in it. High risk. No reward.

So far, what I've been talking about is the difference between choosing technologies that are still on the bleeding edge and technologies that are firmly entrenched. Picking a stable technology that has already wedged itself into the production systems of businesses worldwide is a safer, but potentially less rewarding, choice than picking a flashy new technology that nobody has deployed yet. But, what about the technologies that have run their courses? The ones that are just waiting for the last few nails to be driven into their coffins?

Who drives those nails? You might think of the last few RPG programmers, for example, as being gray-haired and counting the hours until retirement, while the new generation of youngsters haven't even *heard of* RPG. They're all learning Java and .NET. It's easy to imagine that the careers of the last-remaining stalwarts of an aged and dying technology are in the same death spiral as the technology itself.

But, the old systems don't just die. They are replaced. Furthermore, in most cases, homegrown systems are replaced in stages. In those stages, the old systems have to talk to the new systems. Someone has to know how to make the new speak to the old, and vice versa. Typically, the young tykes don't know (or *want* to know) how to make the old systems listen. Nor do the crusty old pre-retirees know how to make the newfangled systems talk to their beloved creatures.

> Both ends of the technology adoption curve might prove to be lucrative.

So, there's a role to be filled by a calculating technologist: *technology hospice*. Helping the old systems die comfortably and with dignity is a task that should not be underestimated. And, of course, most people will jump ship before it sinks, either via retirement or by sidestepping into another technology realm. By being the last one left to support still-critical systems, you can pretty much call the shots. It's risky, in that once the technology *really is* gone, you'll be an expert in something that doesn't exist. However, if you can move fast enough, you can look for the next dying generation of legacy systems and start again.

The adoption curve has edges at either end. How far out on the edges do you want to be?

Act on It!

1. Make a list of early, middle, and late adoption technologies based on today's market. Map them out on paper from left to right; the left is bleeding edge, and the right is filled by technologies that are in their sunsets. Push yourself to find as many technologies in each part of the spectrum as possible. Be as granular as possible about where in the curve they fall in relation to one another.

    When you have as many technologies mapped out as you can think of, mark the ones that you consider yourself strong in. Then, perhaps in a different color, mark the ones that you have some experience with but aren't authoritative on. Where are most of your marks on the adoption curve? Do they clump? Are they spread evenly across? Are there any technologies around the far edges that you have some special interest in?

Supply and Demand

When the Web started to really take off, you could make a lot of money creating simple HTML pages for companies. Every company wanted a web page, and relatively few people knew how to make them. Companies were willing to pay top dollar for "experienced" web designers, which, back then, meant that they knew the basics of HTML, hyperlinking, and site structure.

Making HTML pages is pretty simple. It's hard to make really nice-looking pages, but the basics are easy to grasp. As people observed the prices these web designers were demanding, more and more people started picking up books on HTML and teaching themselves. The market was hot, the salaries or hourly fees were attractive, and the supply of HTML experts started to rise as a response.

As the market flooded with web designers, the web people started to stratify between the truly artistic and the utilitarian. Furthermore, competition started to drive the prices down. As a result of lower prices, more companies were willing to take their first step into an Internet presence. They might not have paid $5,000 for their first website, but they would pay $500.

Of course, some companies were still willing to give up the big bucks for a *fantastic* website. And, certain web designers could still command *fantastic* compensation.

Eventually, the web designer flood at the low-to-middle cost tiers receded. Less talented web designers were replaced by end users and other IT folk who didn't necessarily specialize in HTML design. At this point, the supply, demand, and price of HTML creation reached an equilibrium.

This armchair history of the vocation of web design demonstrates an economic model that we've all heard of, called *supply and demand*. When most of us think of supply and demand, we think that it has to do largely with what price something can and will be sold at. If there are more of an item for sale than the number of people who want to buy that item, then the price of the item will decrease. If there are more people who want the item than there are items available to be purchased, the price of the item will increase as potential buyers compete.

In addition to predicting the prices of goods and services, the supply-and-demand model can predict how price changes will affect the number of people willing to sell and purchase a product or service. There are usually more buyers for any given thing at a lower price than at a higher one.

Why is this important to us? The offshore software trend has just injected a large supply of low-cost IT people into our economy. Though we're worried about losing jobs domestically, the lower

You can't compete on price. In fact, you can't afford to compete on price.

cost per programmer has actually *increased* overall demand. At the same time, as demand increases, price decreases. Competition in high-demand products and services hinges on price. In the employment market, that means salary. You can't compete on price. You can't afford it. So, what do you do?

The offshore market has injected its low-cost programmers into a relatively narrow set of technologies. Java and .NET programmers are a dime a dozen in India. India has a lot of Oracle DBAs as well. Less mainstream technologies are very much underrepresented by the offshore development shops. When choosing a technology set to focus your career on, you should understand the effects of increased supply and lower prices on your career prospects.

As a .NET programmer, you may find yourself competing with tens of thousands of more people in the job market than you would if you were, for example, a Python programmer. This would result in the average cost of a .NET programmer decreasing significantly, possibly driving demand higher (in other words, creating more .NET jobs). So, you'd be likely to find jobs available, but the jobs wouldn't pay all that well. The supply of Python programmers might be much smaller than that of .NET programmers with a demand to match.

If the Python job market were to support noticeably higher prices per programmer, additional people might be attracted to *supply* their services at this higher price range, resulting in competition that would drive the price back down.

The whole thing is a balancing act. But, one thing seems certain (for now). India caters to the already balanced IT services markets. You don't find mainstream Indian offshoring companies jumping on unconventional technologies. They aren't first-movers. They generally don't take chances. They wait for technology services markets to balance, and they disrupt those markets with significantly lower per-programmer costs.

Based on this observation, you might choose to compete in segments of the job market in which there is actually *lower* demand. As unintuitive as that may sound, if you're worried about losing employment to offshoring, one strategy would be to avoid the types of work that offshore companies are doing. Offshore companies are doing work that is in high demand. So, focusing on niche technologies is a strategy that, although not necessarily making the competition less fierce (there are fewer jobs to go around), might change the focus of the competition from price to ability. That's what you need. You can't compete on price, but you *can* compete on ability.

Also, with the *average* price of these mainstream programmers decreasing, the demand will increase. An overall increase in demand for Java programmers, for example, might actually result in *more* jobs (of a certain type) at home, not fewer. An increase in the lower-priced offshore market could drive overall demand, including a higher bracket of developers.

This happens in practice. To make offshoring work well, many companies realize the need for a reserve of high-end, onshore developers who can set standards, ensure quality, and provide technical leadership. An increase in overall Java programming demand would naturally lead to an increase in this category of Java work. The low-end jobs might be going offshore, but there are more of the elite jobs to go around than there were pre-offshoring. As we saw in the niche job markets, in this tier of Java development work, the competition would shift from price to ability.

Exploit market imbalances. The most important lesson we can learn from the supply and demand model is that with increased demand comes increased price competition. The tried-and-true, follow-the-jobs strategy will put you squarely in price competition with offshore developers, because your skills will fit into the offshore-friendly balanced markets. To compete in the mainstream technology market, you'll have to compete at a higher tier. Alternatively, you could exploit market *imbalances*—going where the offshore companies won't go. In either case, it pays to understand the forces at work and to be skilled and nimble enough to react to them.

Act on It!

1. Research current technical skill demand. Use job posting and career websites to find out which skills are in high demand and in low demand. Find the websites of some offshore outsourcing companies (or talk to employees of those companies if you work with them). Compare the skills available via these companies with the high-demand list you compiled. Make note of which skills appear to be in high demand domestically with little penetration offshore.

   Do a similar comparison between leading-edge technologies and the skills available via offshore outsourcing firms. Keep your eyes on both sets of technical skills that are underserved by the offshore companies. How long does it take for them to fill the holes (if ever)? This time gap is the window during which a market imbalance exists.

Coding Don't Cut It Anymore

It's not enough to think about what technologies you're going to invest in. After all, the technology part is a commodity, right? You're not going to be able to sit back and simply master a programming language or an operating system, letting the businesspeople take care of the business stuff. If all they needed was a code robot, it would be easy to hire someone in another country to do that kind of work. If you want to stay relevant, you're going to have to dive into the domain of the business you're in.

In fact, a software person should understand a business domain not only well enough to develop software for it but also to become one of its authorities. At a previous company, I saw an excellent example of this. The database administration team consisted of people who really weren't interested in database technology. When I was first exposed to them, it was a bit of a shock. *Why are these people in information technology?* I wondered. In terms of technical skill, they just weren't very strong. But, this team had something special. Being the keepers and protectors of our enterprise data, they actually knew the business domain better than almost any business analyst we had. Their knowledge and understanding of the business made them hot commodities in the internal job posting market. While us geeks were looking at them disdainfully, the *business* for which they worked recognized a ton of value in them.

You should think of your business domain experience as an important part of your repertoire. If you're a musician, when you add something to your repertoire, it doesn't just mean you've played the song once. It means you truly *know* the song. You should apply the same theory to your business domain experience. For example, having worked on a project in the health insurance industry doesn't guarantee that you understand the difference between an HIPAA 835 and an HIPAA 837 EDI transaction. It's this kind of knowledge that differentiates two otherwise equivalent software developers in the right situation.

You might be "just a programmer," but being able to speak to your business clients in the language of their business domain is a critical skill. Imagine how much easier life would be if everyone you had to work with really understood how software development works. You wouldn't have to explain to them why it's a bad idea to return 30,000 records in a single page on a web application or why they shouldn't pass out links to your development server. This is how your business clients feel about you: *Imagine how much easier it would be to work with these programmers if they just understood what I was asking them for without me having to dumb everything down and be so ridiculously specific!* And, guess what? It's the business that pays your salary.

Just like technologies that become hot, business domains can be selected in the same way. Java and .NET are the Big Things right now in software development. If you learn them, you can compete for a job in one of the many companies that will employ these technologies. The same is true of business domains. You should put the same level of care into selecting which industry to serve as you put into selecting which technologies to master.

In light of the importance that you should place on selecting a business domain when rounding out your portfolio, the company and industry you choose to work for

> Now is the time to think about business domains you invest your time in.

becomes a significant investment on your part. If you haven't yet given real, intentional thought to which business domains you should be investing in, now is the time. Each passing day is a missed opportunity. Like leaving your savings in a low-yield savings account when higher interest rates are to be had, leaving your development on the business front in stasis is a bad investment choice.

Act on It!

1. Schedule lunch with a businessperson. Talk to them about how they do their job. As you talk to them, ask yourself what you would have to change or learn if you aspired to have their job. Ask about the specifics of their daily work. Talk to them about how technology helps them (or slows them down) on the job. Think about *your* work from their perspective.

   Do this regularly.

   This may seem like an awkward or uncomfortable idea. That's OK. I started doing this several years ago, and it made a huge difference in the way I understood and related to the business I was supporting.

I also got more comfortable talking to my customers, which is a positive side effect.

2.   Pick up a trade magazine for your company's industry. You probably don't even have to buy one. Most companies have back issues of trade rags lying around somewhere. Start trying to work your way through a magazine. You may not understand everything you read, but be persistent. Make lists of questions you can ask your management or business clients. Even if your questions seem stupid to you, your business clients will appreciate that you are trying to learn.

Look for industry websites that you can monitor on a regular basis. In both the websites and the magazines, pay special attention to what the big news items and the feature articles are about. What is your industry struggling with? What's the hot new issue right now? Whatever it is, bring it up with your business clients. Ask them to explain it and to give you their opinions. Think about how these current trends affect *your* company, your division, your team, and eventually your work.

Be the Worst

Legendary jazz guitarist Pat Metheny has a stock piece of advice for young musicians, which is "Always be the worst guy in every band you're in."[2]

Before starting my career in information technology, I was a professional jazz and blues saxophonist. As a musician, I had the good fortune of learning this lesson early on and sticking to it. Being the worst guy in the band means always playing with people who are better than you.

> Be the worst guy in every band you're in.

Now, why would you always choose to be the worst person in a band? "Isn't it unnerving?" you ask. Yes, it's extremely unnerving at first. As a young musician, I would find myself in situations where I was so obviously the worst guy in the band that I was *sure* I would stick out like a sore thumb. I'd show up to a gig and not even want to unpack my saxophone for fear I'd be forcefully ejected from the bandstand. I'd find myself standing next to people I looked up to, expected to perform at their level—sometimes as the lead instrument!

Without fail (thankfully!), something magical would happen in these situations: I would fit in. I wouldn't stand out among the other musicians as a star. On the other hand, I wouldn't be obviously outclassed, either. This would happen for two reasons. The first reason is that I really wasn't as bad as I thought. We'll come back to this one later.

The more interesting reason that I would fit in with these superior musicians—my heroes, in some cases—is that my playing would transform itself to be more like theirs. I'd like to think I had some kind of superhuman ability to morph into a genius simply by standing next to one, but in retrospect I think it's a lot less glamorous than that. It was more like some kind of instinctual herd behavior, programmed into me. It's the same phenomenon that makes me

---

2. Originally spotted by Chris Morris at http://clabs.org/blogki.

adopt new vocabulary or grammatical habits when I'm around people who speak differently than me. When we returned from a year and a half of living in India, my wife would sometimes listen to me speaking and burst into laughter, "Did you *hear* what you just said?" I was speaking Indian English.

Being the worst guy in the band brought out the same behavior in me as a saxophonist. I would naturally just play like everyone else. What makes this phenomenon really unglamorous is that when I played in casinos and hole-in-the-wall bars with those not-so-good bands, I played like *those* guys. Also, like an alcoholic who slurs his speech even when he's not drunk, I'd find the bad habits of the bar bands carrying over to my non-bar-band nights.

So, I learned from this that people can significantly improve or regress in skill, purely based on who they are performing with. And, prolonged experience with a group can have a lasting impact on one's ability to perform.

> The people around you affect your own performance. Choose your crowd wisely.

Later, as I moved into the computer industry, I found that this learned habit of seeking out the best musicians came naturally to me as a programmer. Perhaps unconsciously, I sought out the best IT people to work with. And, not surprisingly, the lesson holds true. Being the worst guy (or gal, of course) on the team has the same effect as being the worst guy in the band. You find that you're unexplainably *smarter*. You even speak and write more intelligently. Your code and designs get more elegant, and you find that you're able to solve hard problems with increasingly creative solutions.

Let's go back to the first reason that I was able to blend into those bands better than I expected. I really wasn't as bad as I thought. In music, it's pretty easy to measure whether other musicians think you're good. If you're good, they invite you to play with them again. If you're not, they avoid you. It's a much more reliable measurement than just asking them what they think, because good musicians don't like playing with bad ones. Much to my surprise, I found that in many cases, I would get called by one or more of these superior musicians for additional work or to even start bands with them.

Attempting to be the worst actually stops you from selling yourself short. You might belong in the A band but always put yourself in the B band, because you're afraid. Acknowledging outright that you're not the best wipes away the fear of being discovered for the not-best person you are. In reality, even when you *try* to be the worst, you won't actually be.

Act on It!

1. Find a "be the worst" situation for yourself. You may not have the luxury of immediately switching teams or companies just because you want to work with better people. Instead, find a volunteer project on which you can work with other developers who will make you better via osmosis. Check for developer group meetings in your city, and attend those meetings. Developers are often looking for spare-time projects on which to practice new techniques and hone their skills.

    If you don't have an active developer community nearby, use the Internet. Pick an open source project that you admire and whose developers appear to be at that "next level" you're looking to reach. Go through the project's to-do list or mailing list archives, pick a feature or a major bug fix, and code away! Emulate the style of the project's surrounding code. Turn it into a game. Make your design and code so indistinguishable from the rest of the project that even the original developers eventually won't remember who wrote it. Then, when you're satisfied with your work, submit it as a patch. If it's good, it will be accepted into the project. Start over, and do it again. If you've made decisions that the project's developers disagree with, either incorporate their feedback and resubmit or take note of the changes they make. On your next patch, try to get it in with less rework. Eventually, you'll find yourself to be a trusted member of the project team. You'll be amazed at what you can learn from a remote set of senior developers, even if you never get a chance to hear their voices.

Invest in Your Intelligence

When choosing what to focus on, it can be tempting to simply look at the technologies that yield the most jobs and focus on those. Java is big. .NET is big. Learning Java has a simple, transitive effect: if I know Java, I can apply for, and possibly get, a job writing Java code.

Using this logic, it would be foolish to choose to invest in a niche technology, especially if you had no plans to try to exploit that niche.

TIOBE Software uses Internet search engines to indicate the relative popularity of programming languages, based on people talking about those languages on the Internet.[3] According to TIOBE's website, "The ratings are based on the worldwide availability of skilled engineers, courses, and third-party vendors." It's definitely not a scientifically provable measure of popularity, but it's a pretty good indicator.

At the time of writing, the most popular language is Java, followed by C. C# is in a respectable sixth place but with a slight upward trajectory. SAP's ABAP is in seventeenth place and is moving slowly downward. Ruby, which is my personal favorite programming language—the one I do pretty much all of my *serious* work in and the one for which I co-organize an international conference every year—is in eleventh place. But at the time the first edition of this book was published, it wasn't even in the top twenty. It was below ABAP!

Was I crazy to use Ruby or just stupid? I must be one of the two, right?

In his essay "Great Hackers,"[4] Paul Graham annoyed the industry with the assertion that Java programmers aren't as smart as Python programmers. He made a lot of stupid Java programmers mad (did I say that?), causing a lot of them to write counterarguments on their websites. The violent reaction indicates that he touched a nerve. I was in the audience when his essay was first presented, in the form of a speech. For me, it sparked a flashback.

---

3.   http://www.tiobe.com/index.php/content/paperinfo/tpci/index.html
4.   http://paulgraham.com/gh.html

I was on a recruiting trip in India weeding through hundreds of candidates for only tens of jobs, and the interview team was exhausting itself and running out of time because of a poor interview-to-hire hit rate. Heads hurting and eyes red, we held a late-night meeting to discuss a strategic change in the way we would go through the candidates. We had to either optimize the process so we could interview more people or somehow interview *better* people (or both). With what little was left of my voice after twelve straight hours of trying to drag answers out of dumbstruck programmers, I argued for adding Smalltalk to the list of keywords our headhunters were using to search their résumé database. "But, nobody knows Smalltalk in India," cried the human resources director. That was my point. Nobody knew it, and programming in Smalltalk was a fundamentally different experience than programming in Java. The varying experience would give candidates a different level of expectations, and the dynamic nature of the Smalltalk environment would reshape the way a Java programmer would approach a problem. My hope was that these factors would encourage a level of technical maturity that I hadn't been seeing from the candidates I'd met so far.

The addition of Smalltalk to the requirements list yielded a candidate pool that was tiny in contrast to our previous list. These people were diamonds in the rough. They really understood object-oriented programming. They were aware that Java isn't the idealistic panacea it's sometimes made out to be. Many of them *loved* to program! *Where have you been for the past two weeks?* we thought.

Unfortunately, our ability to attract these developers for the salaries we were able to pay was limited. They were calling the shots, and most of them chose to stay where they were or to keep looking for a new job. Though we failed to recruit many of them, we learned a valuable recruiting lesson: we were more likely to extend offers to candidates with diverse (and even unorthodox) experience than to those whose experiences were homogenous. My explanation is that either good people seek out diversity, because they love to learn new things, *or* being forced into alien experiences and environments created more mature, well-rounded software developers. I suspect it's a little of both, but regardless of *why* it works, we learned that it works. I still use this technique when looking for developers.

So, other than trying to show up on *my* radar screen when I'm looking to hire someone, why else would you want to invest in fringe technologies that you may rarely or never have an opportunity to actually get paid to use?

For me, as a hiring manager, the first reason is that it shows that you're interested. If I *know* you learned something for the sake of self-development and (better) pure fun, I know you are excited and motivated about your profession. It drives me crazy to ask people whether they've seen or used certain not-quite-mainstream technologies only to hear, "I haven't been given the opportunity to work on that" in return. *Given* the opportunity? Neither was I! I *took* the opportunity to learn.

> *I haven't been given the opportunity…?*
>
> Seize the opportunity!

More important than portraying the perception of being suitably motivated and engaged by your field is that exposure to these fringe technologies and methodologies actually makes you deeper, better, smarter, and more creative.

If that's not good enough reason, then you're probably in the wrong profession.

Act on It!

1. Learn a new programming language. But, don't go from Java to C# or from C to C++. Learn a new language that makes you think in a new way. If you're a Java or C# programmer, try learning a language like Smalltalk or Ruby that doesn't employ strong, static typing. Or, if you've been doing object-oriented programming for a long time, try a functional language like Haskell or Scheme. You don't *have* to become an expert. Work through enough code that you truly feel the difference in the new programming environment. If it doesn't feel strange enough, either you've picked the wrong language or you're applying your old way of thinking to the new language. Go out of your way to learn the idioms of the new language. Ask old-timers to review your code and make suggestions that would make it more idiomatically correct.

Don't Listen to Your Parents

In our culture, there's something sacred about following the advice of your parents. It's seen as a child's duty and ranks up there with doing one's religious duty as The Right Thing to do. Books, movies, and television plots are hinged on the parents' wisdom as a moral. But for careers in our industry, this moral is wrong.

Your parents would rather you be OK than have a remarkable career at the cost of great personal risk. More than any other third party you might look to, your parents are going to give you fear-driven advice. Fear-driven advice is geared toward *not losing*. Thinking about not losing is *not* the way to win! Winners take risks. They think about where they want to go—not where the rest of the pack is. Fear-driven career planning is more likely to land you in a cubicle farm for the rest of your life than on the path to greatness. Sure, it's safe, but it's no fun.

A generation ago, fun wasn't a deciding factor when we talked about career choices. Jobs aren't supposed to be fun. They're supposed to bring home the bacon. Fun is what you do on your off days. Fun happens in the evenings and weekends. But if your job isn't fun, as we've come to realize, you don't do a *fantastic* job at it. It's not so much that things are different now, but our cultural understanding of what it means to work has shifted for the better. More of us understand that passion leads to excellence. And without fun, there's unlikely to be any passion in a software job.

Another career decision-making factor that is likely not in line with your parents' view of the working world is that it's OK (and often preferable) to change jobs. A well-rounded software professional has seen many angles of the industry: product development, IT support, internal business systems development, and government work. The more domains you've seen and the more technical architectures you've slogged through, the more prepared you are to make the right decisions on tougher projects. Staying in a single company, working your way up the ranks, is a limiting environment in which to grow as a developer. Gone are the days of the "lifer" who would join a big company and settle in for a full career. This sort of behavior used to be a sign of dedication. Now it's a liability. If you've worked in only one place and seen one set of systems, many (smart) managers would see that as a strike against you when making a hiring decision. I'd personally rather hire someone who has seen a variety of successes and failures in different environments than someone who has known only one way of doing things.

Several years ago, I realized that my career had been informed too much by the professional values of my parents and their generation. I worked for one of the world's largest and most stable corporations and was upwardly mobile at a slow and steady pace. But I was stagnating. I had reassured myself that I wasn't pigeon-holing myself based on the fact that the corporation was so large I could do lots of different jobs in a seemingly limitless list of locations. But I ultimately stayed in the same place doing the same kind of work.

I remember talking to a friend about potentially moving out of this company, and he said, "Is it your destiny to work at $big_company for the rest of your life?" *Hell no it wasn't!* So, I quickly found another job and left.

This movement marked the clear beginning of a nonlinear jump in my success in the software industry. I saw new domains, I worked on harder problems, and I was rewarded more heavily than ever before. It was scary at times, but when I decided to be less fear-driven and conservative in my career choice, the shape and tone of my career—my life—changed for the better.

Take calculated risks with your career. Don't let fear consume you. And if you're not having fun, you're not going to be excellent.

Act on It!

1. What are your biggest career fears? Think about the last few career choices you made. They don't have to be big decisions (after all, if you're making fear-driven choices, your decisions likely aren't big anyway). They could be whether you took on special assignments or whether you applied for a job change or promotion. Make a list of these choices, and, for each one, force yourself to make an honest assessment: how much was your decision driven by fear? What would you have done if fear had not been a factor? If the decision was indeed fear-driven, how can you reverse it or find a similar opportunity in which to make the less fear-driven choice?

How I Turned Down $300,000 from Microsoft to Go Full-Time on GitHub

by Tom Preston-Werner

2008 is a leap year. That means that 366 days ago, almost to the minute, I was sitting alone in a booth at Zeke's Sports Bar and Grill on Third Street in San Francisco. I wouldn't normally hang out at a sports bar, let alone a sports bar in SOMA, but back then Thursday was "I Can Has Ruby" night. I guess back then "I can has _" was also a reasonable moniker to attach to pretty much anything. ICHR was a semiprivate meeting of like-minded Ruby hackers that generally and willingly devolved into late-night drinking sessions. Normally these nights would fade away like my hangover the next morning, but this night was different. This was the night that GitHub was born.

I think I was sitting at the booth alone because I'd just ordered a fresh Fat Tire and needed a short break from the socializing that was happening over at the long tables in the dimly lit back portion of the bar. On the fifth or sixth sip, Chris Wanstrath walked in. I have trouble remembering now if I'd even classify Chris and I as "friends" at the time. We knew each other through Ruby meet-ups and conferences but only casually. Like a mutual "Hey, I think your code is awesome" kind of thing. I'm not sure what made me do it, but I gestured him over to the booth and said, "Dude, check this out." About a week earlier I'd started work on a project called Grit that allowed me to access Git repositories in an object-oriented manner via Ruby code. Chris was one of only a handful of Rubyists at the time who was starting to become serious about Git. He sat down, and I started showing him what I had. It wasn't much, but it was enough to see that it had sparked something in Chris. Sensing this, I launched into my half-baked idea for some sort of website that acted as hub for coders to share their Git repositories. I even had a name: GitHub. I may be paraphrasing, but his response was along the lines of a very emphatic "I'm in. Let's do it!"

The next night—Friday, October 19, 2007, at 10:24 p.m.—Chris made the first commit to the GitHub repository and sealed in digital stone the beginning of our joint venture.

How I Turned Down $300,000 from Microsoft (continued)

There were, so far, no agreements of any kind regarding how things would proceed. We were just two guys who decided to hack together on something that sounded cool.

Remember those amazing few minutes in *Karate Kid* where Daniel is training to become a martial arts expert? Remember the music? Well, you should probably go buy and listen to *You're the Best* by Joe Esposito in iTunes because I'm about to hit you with a montage.

For the next three months Chris and I spent ridiculous hours planning and coding GitHub. I kept going with Grit and designed the UI. Chris built out the Rails app. We met in person every Saturday to make design decisions and try to figure out what the hell our pricing plan would look like. I remember one very rainy day we talked for a good two hours about various pricing strategies over some of the best Vietnamese egg rolls in the city. All of this we did while holding other engagements. I, for one, was employed full-time at Powerset as a tools developer for the Ranking and Relevance team.

In mid-January, after three months of nights and weekends, we launched into private beta mode, sending invites to our friends. In mid-February, P.J. Hyett joined in and made us three-strong. We publicly launched the site on April 10. TechCrunch was not invited. At this point, it was still just three 20-somethings without a single penny of outside investment.

I was still working full-time at Powerset on July 1, 2008, when we learned that Powerset had just been acquired by Microsoft for around $100 million. This was interesting timing. With the acquisition, I was going to be faced with a choice sooner than I had anticipated. I could either sign on as a Microsoft employee or quit and go GitHub full-time. At 29 years old, I was the oldest of the three GitHubbers and had accumulated a proportionally larger amount of debt and monthly expenditure. I was used to my six-digit lifestyle. Further confounding the issue was the imminent return of my wife, Theresa, from her PhD fieldwork in Costa Rica. I would soon be transitioning from make-believe bachelor back to married man.

How I Turned Down $300,000 from Microsoft (continued)

To muddy the waters of decision even more, the Microsoft employment offer was juicy. Salary plus $300,000 over three years juicy. That's enough money to make anybody think twice about anything. So, I was faced with this: a safe job with lots of guaranteed money as a Microsoft man *or* a risky job with unknown amounts of money as an entrepreneur. I knew things with the other GitHub guys would become extremely strained if I stayed on at Powerset much longer. Having saved up some money and become freelancers some time ago, they had both started dedicating full-time effort to GitHub. It was "do or die" time. Either pick GitHub and go for it or make the safe choice and quit GitHub to make wheelbarrows full of cash at Microsoft.

If you want a recipe for restless sleep, I can give you one. Add one part "What will my wife think?" with 3,000 parts Benjamin Franklin, stir in a "beer any time you damn well please," and top it with a chance at financial independence.

I've become pretty good at giving my employers the bad news that I'm leaving the company to go do something cooler. I broke the news to my boss at Powerset on the day the employment offer was due. I told him I was quitting to go work full-time on GitHub. Like any great boss, he was bummed but understanding. He didn't try to tempt me with a bigger bonus or anything. I think deep down he knew I was going to leave. I may have even received a larger incentive to stay than others, on account of my being a flight risk. Those Microsoft managers are crafty, I tell you. They have retention bonuses down to a science—well, except when you throw an entrepreneur, the singularity of the business world, into the mix. Everything goes wacky when you have one of those around.

In the end, just as Indiana Jones could never turn down the opportunity to search for the Holy Grail, I could no less turn down the chance to work for myself on something I truly love, no matter how safe the alternative might be. When I'm old and dying, I plan to look back on my life and say, "Wow, that was an adventure," not "Wow, I sure felt safe."

Tom Preston-Werner is cofounder of GitHub.

Be a Generalist

For at least a couple of decades, desperate managers and business owners have been pretending that software development is a manufacturing process at heart. Requirements specifications are created, and architects turn these specifications into a high-level technical vision. Designers fill out the architecture with detailed design documentation, which is then handed to robot-like coders, who hold their pulp-fiction novels in one hand while sleepily typing in the design's implementation with the other. Finally, Inspector 12 receives the completed code, which doesn't receive her stamp of approval unless it meets the original specifications.

It's no surprise that managers want software development to be like manufacturing. Managers *understand* how to make manufacturing work. We have decades of experience in how to build physical objects efficiently and accurately. So, applying what we've learned from manufacturing, we should be able to optimize the software development process into the well-tuned engine that our manufacturing plants have become.

In the so-called software factory, the employees are specialists. They sit at their place in the assembly line, fastening Java components together or rounding the rough edges of a Visual Basic application on their software lathes. Inspector 12 is a tester by trade. Software components move down the line, and she tests and stamps them in the same way each day. J2EE designers design J2EE applications. C++ coders code in C++. The world is very clean and compartmentalized.

Unfortunately, the manufacturing analogy doesn't work. Software is at least as malleable as software requirements. Things change in business, and businesspeople know that software is *soft* and can be changed to meet those requirements. This means architecture, designs, code, and tests must all be created and revised in a fashion more agile than the leanest manufacturing processes can provide.

In this kind of rapidly changing environment, the flexible will excel. When the pressure is on, a smart businessperson will turn to a software professional who can solve the problem at hand. So, how do you become that person whose name comes up when they're looking for a superhero to save the day? The key is to be able to solve the problems that may arise.

What are those problems? That's right: you don't know. Neither do I. What I *do* know is that those problems are as diverse as deployment issues, critical design flaws that need to be solved and quickly reimplemented, heterogeneous system integration, and ad hoc report generation. Faced with a problem set as diverse as this, poor Inspector 12 would be passed over pretty quickly.

The label "jack-of-all-trades but master of none" is normally meant to be derogatory, implying that the labelee lacks the focus to really dive into a subject and master it. But, when your online shopping application is on the fritz and you're losing orders by the hundreds as each hour passes, it's the jack-of-all-trades who not only knows how the application's code works but can also do low-level UNIX debugging of your web server processes, analyze your RDBMS's configuration for potential performance bottlenecks, and check your network's router configuration for hard-to-find problems. And, more important, after finding the problem, the jack-of-all-trades can quickly make architecture and design decisions, implement code fixes, and deploy a new fixed system to production. In this scenario, the manufacturing scenario seems quaint at best and critically flawed at worst.

Another way in which the software factory breaks down is in that, in contrast to an assembly line where the work keeps coming in a steady flow, software projects are usually very cyclical. Not only is the actual flow of projects cyclical, but the work inside a project is cyclical. A coder sits on the bench while requirements are being specified, architected, and designed, or the coder multitasks across many projects. The problem with multitasking coders is that, despite the software factory's intentions, when the rubber meets the road, the coders rely a great deal on context and experience to get their jobs done. Requirements, architecture, and design documents can be a great head start, but ultimately if the programmers don't understand what the system is supposed to do, they won't be able to create a good implementation of the system.

Of course, I'm not just picking on coders here. The same is true at nearly every spot on the software assembly line. Context matters, and multitasking doesn't quite work. As a result, we have an inefficient manufacturing system. There have been various attempts to solve this problem of inefficiency without departing from the manufacturing-inspired system, but we have not yet figured out how to optimize our software factories to an acceptable level.

If you are *just* a coder or a tester or a designer or an architect, you're going to find yourself sitting idle or doing busywork during the ebbs of your business's project flow. If you are *just* a J2EE programmer or a .NET programmer or a UNIX systems programmer, you're not going to have much to contribute when the focus of a project or a company shifts, even temporarily, out of your focus area. It's not about where you sit on the perceived value chain of project work (where the architect holds the highest spot of royalty). It's about how generally useful you make yourself.

If your goal is to be the last person standing amid rounds of layoffs and the shipment of jobs overseas, you better make yourself *generally* useful. If you're afraid that your once-crowded development office will become home to an onshore skeleton crew, it would serve you well to realize that when the team has only a few slots, a "just-a-tester" or "just-a-coder" is not going to be in demand. Better, if you just want to stand out and be remarkable, wrapping your head around The Big Picture is where it's at.

> Generalists are rare...and, therefore, precious.

The way to become a generalist is to not label yourself with a specific role or technology. We can become typecast in our careers in many ways. To visualize what it means to be a generalist, it can help to dissect the IT career landscape into its various independent aspects. I can think of five, but an infinite number exists (it's all in how you personally divide topics):

- Rung on the career ladder
- Platform/OS
- Code vs. data
- Systems vs. applications
- Business vs. IT

These are different dimensions on which you can approach the problem of becoming a generalist. This is just a way to think about the whole picture of your career, and you can probably come up with a better list for yourself. For now, we'll discuss these.

First, you can choose to either be a leader or manager type or be a technical person. Or, you might pigeonhole yourself into architect as opposed to being a programmer or tester. The ability to be flexible in the roles you can and will fill is an attribute that many people don't understand the value of. For example, while a strong leader should avoid pinch-hitting as often as possible, the new world of onshore skeleton crews can benefit from a person who knows how to lead people and projects but can also roll up their sleeves and fix some last-minute critical bugs while the offshore team is sleeping. The same is true of a software architect who could perhaps dramatically speed up progress on a project if he or she would only *write some code* to get things moving. When it comes to hierarchical boundary crossing, it's most often not reluctance that stops people from doing it. It's ability. Programmer geeks can't lead, and leaders can't hack. It's rare to find someone who's even decent at both.

Another artificial (and inexcusable) line gets drawn around platforms or operating systems. Being a UNIX Guy who refuses to do Windows is increasingly more impractical. The same goes for .NET vs. J2EE or any other such infrastructure platforms. Longevity is going to require that you are platform neutral in the workplace. We all have our preferences, but you're going to have to leave your ideals at home. Master one, and get good at the other. Your skills should transcend technology platform. It's just a tool. If we want a Windows person, we can hire them in the Philippines. If we want someone who really understands Windows and UNIX development and can help us integrate them together, we're probably going to be looking onshore. Don't get passed up because of what is essentially team spirit.

> Your skills should transcend technology platforms.

The dividing line between database administrator (a role that has solidified out of nothingness over the past decade) and software developer should also be fuzzy. Being a database administrator, or DBA, has in many organizations come to mean that you know how to use some GUI admin tool and you know how to set up a specific database product. You don't necessarily know much of anything about how to *use* the database. On the flip side, software developers are growing increasingly lazy and ignorant about how to work with databases. Each side feeds the other.

What first amazed me most when I entered the information technology field was that many well-educated programmers (maybe *most*) didn't know the first thing about how to set up the systems they used for development and deployment. I worked with developers who couldn't even install an operating system on a PC if you asked them to, much less set up an application server on which to deploy their applications. It's rare, and refreshing, to find a developer who truly understands the platform on which he or she is working. Applications are better and work gets done faster as a result.

Finally, as we discussed in Tip 3, *Coding Don't Cut It Anymore,* on page 13, the wall between The Business and IT should be torn down right now. Start learning how your business operates.

Act on It!

1. On a piece of paper or a whiteboard, list the dimensions on which you may or may not be generalizing your knowledge and abilities. For each dimension, write your specialty. For example, if *Platform and Operating System* is one of your dimensions, you might write *Windows/.NET* next to it. Now, to the right of your specialty, write one or more topics you should put into your "To Learn" list. Continuing with the same example, you might write *Linux* and *Java* (or even *Ruby* or *Perl*).

    As soon as possible (some time this week at the latest!), find thirty minutes of time to start addressing at least one of the "To Learn" items on your list. Don't just read about it. If possible, get some hands-on experience. If it's web technology, then download a web server package and set it up yourself. If it's a business topic, find one of your customers at work and ask them to go out for lunch for a chat.

Be a Specialist

"How would you write a program, in pure Java, that would make the Java Virtual Machine crash?" Dead silence. "Hello?"

"I'm sorry. I'm not getting you. Could you repeat the question, please?" The voice sounded desperate. I knew from experience that repeating the question wasn't going to help. So, I repeated the question, slowly and more loudly. "How would you write a program, in pure Java, that would cause the Java Virtual Machine to crash?"

"Uh…I'm sorry. I've never done that before."

"I'm sure you haven't. How about this question: how would you write a program that would NOT cause the JVM to crash?"

I was looking for really good Java programmers. To start the interview, I asked this person (and all the others I had interviewed that week) to rate himself on a scale of one to ten. He said *nine*. I'm expecting a star here. If this guy rates himself so high, why can't he think of a single abusive programming trick that would cause a JVM to crash?

Lack of technical depth.

This was someone who claimed to specialize in Java. If you met him at a party and asked what he did for a living, he would say, "I am a Java developer." Yet, he couldn't answer this simple question. He couldn't even come up with a

> Too many of us seem to believe that specializing in something simply means not knowing about other things.

wrong answer. Over two-and-a-half intense weeks of interviewing on a cross-country recruiting trip, this was the rule—not the exception. Thousands of Java specialists had applied for open positions, nearly none of whom could explain how a Java class loader works or give a high-level overview of how memory management is typically handled by a Java Virtual Machine.

Granted, you don't have to know all these things to hack out basic code under the supervision of others. But, these were supposed to be *experts*.

Too many of us seem to believe that specializing in something simply means you don't know about other things. I could, for example, call my mother a Windows specialist, because she has never used Linux or OS X. Or, I could say that my relatives out in the countryside in Arkansas are country music specialists, because they've never heard anything else.

Imagine you visit your family doctor, complaining about a strange lump under the skin of your right arm. Your doctor refers you to a specialist to have a biopsy performed. What if that specialist was a person whose only credentials as a specialist were that they didn't attend any classes in medical school or have any experience in residencies that weren't *directly* relevant to the act of performing the specific procedure that they were going to perform on you today? I don't mean that they went *deeper* into the topics related to today's procedure. What if they had just skimmed the surface of these topics, but they didn't know anything else? "What if that machine over there starts beeping during the operation?" you might ask. "Oh, that's never happened before. It won't happen this time. I don't know what that machine does, but it never beeps."

Thankfully, *most* software developers aren't responsible for life-or-death situations. If they happen to mess up, it typically results in project overruns or production bugs that simply cost their employers money, not lives.

Unfortunately, the software industry has churned out a whole lot of these shallow specialists, who use the term *specialist* as an excuse for knowing only one thing. In the medical industry, a specialist is someone with a *deep* understanding of some specific area of the field. Doctors refer their patients to specialists, because in certain specific circumstances, the specialist can give them better care than a general practitioner.

So, what should a specialist be in the software field? I can tell you what I was searching for in every nook and cranny on that recruiting trip. I was searching for people who deeply understood the Java programming and deployment environment. I wanted folks who could say "been there, done that" in 80 percent of the situations we might encounter and whose depth of knowledge could make the remaining 20 percent more livable. I wanted someone who, when dealing with high-level abstractions, would also understand the low-level details of what went into the implementation of those abstractions. I wanted someone who could solve any deployment issue we might encounter or would at least know who to call for help if they couldn't.

This is the kind of specialist who will survive in the changing computer industry. If you're a .NET specialist, it's not just an excuse for not knowing anything *except* .NET. It means that if it has to do with .NET, you are the authority. IIS servers hanging and needing to be rebooted? "No problem." Source control integration with Visual Studio .NET? "I'll show you how." Customers threatening to pull the plug because of obscure performance issues? "Give me thirty minutes."

If this isn't what *specialist* means to you, then I hope you don't claim to be one.

Act on It!

1. Do you use a programming language that compiles and runs on a virtual machine? If so, take some time to learn about the internals of how your VM works. For Java, .NET, and Smalltalk, many books and websites are devoted to the topic. It's easier to learn about than you think.

    Whether your language relies on a VM or not, take some time to study just what happens when you compile a source file. How does the code you type go from being text that you can read to instructions that a computer can execute? What would it mean to write your own compiler?

    When you import or use external libraries, where do they come from? What does it *actually* mean to import an external library? How does your compiler, operating system, or virtual machine link multiple pieces of code together to form a coherent system?

    Learning these facts will take you several steps closer to being an expert specialist in your technology of choice.

2. Find an opportunity—at work or outside—to teach a class on some aspect of a technology that you would like to develop some depth in. As you'll see in on page 56, teaching is one of the best ways to learn.

Don't Put All Your Eggs in Someone Else's Basket

While managing an application development group, I once asked one of my employees, "What do you want to do with your career? What do you want to be?" I was terribly disappointed by his answer: "I want to be a J2EE architect." I asked why not a "Microsoft Word designer" or a "RealPlayer installer?"

This guy wanted to build his *career* around a specific technology created by a specific company of which he *was not an employee*. What if the company goes out of business? What if it let its now-sexy technology become obsolete? Why would you want to trust a technology company with your career?

Somehow, as an industry, we fool ourselves into thinking *market leader* is the same thing as *standard*. So, to some people, it seems rational to make another company's product part of their identities. Even worse, some base their careers around non-market-leading products—at least until their careers fail so miserably that they have no choice but to rethink this losing strategy.

Let's take a moment again to remember that we should think of our career as a business. Though it's possible to build a business that exists as a parasite of another (such as companies who build spyware removal products to make up for inadequacies in Microsoft's browser security model), as an individual it's an incredibly risky thing to do. A company, such as the spyware example I just mentioned, can usually react to changing forces in the market such as an unexpected improvement in Microsoft's browser security (or Microsoft deciding to enter the spyware removal market), whereas an individual doesn't have the bandwidth or the surplus cash to suddenly change career direction or focus.

Vendor-centric views are typically myopic. The sad thing about a vendor-centric view of the world is that, usually, the details of a vendor's software implementation are a secret. You can really learn only so much about a piece of proprietary software until you reach the *professional services barrier*. The professional services barrier is the artificial barrier that a company erects between you and the solution to a problem you may have so that it can profit from selling you support services. Sometimes this barrier is intentionally erected, and sometimes it's erected as a side effect of the attempt the company makes to protect its intellectual property (by not sharing its source code).

So, although a single-minded investment in one particular technology is almost always a *bad idea*, if you *must* do so, consider focusing on an open source option, as opposed to a commercial one. Even if you can't or don't want to make the case for using the open source solution in your workplace, use the open source option as the platform from which you can take a deep dive into a technology. For example, you may want to become an expert in how J2EE application servers work. Instead of focusing your efforts on the details of how to configure and deploy a commercial application server (after all, *anybody* can figure out how to tweak settings in a config file, right?), download the open source JBoss or Geronimo servers, and set aside time for yourself to not only learn how to operate the servers but to study their internals.

Before long, you'll realize you're naturally changing your view. This J2EE thing (or whatever you chose to get into) really isn't all that special. Now that you see the details of the implementation, you see that there are high-level conceptual patterns at work. And, you start to realize that, whether with Java or some other language or platform, distributed enterprise architecture is distributed enterprise architecture. Your view changes from narrow to wide, and your mind starts to open. You start to realize that these concepts and patterns that your brain is sorting through and making sense of are much more scalable and universal than any specific vendor's technology. "Let the vendors come and go—I know how to design a system!"

Act on It!

1. Try a small project, twice. Try it once in your home base technology and then once, as idiomatically as possible, in a competing technology.

Love It or Leave It

It may sound like some kind of rah-rah cheerleader crap, aimed at whipping you into an idealistic frenzy, but it's too important not to mention. You have to be passionate about your work if you want to be *great* at your work. If you don't care, it will show.

When my wife and I moved to Bangalore, I was really excited. For the first time in my career, I was looking forward to finding nearby like-minded technologists with a passion for learning. I was expecting a vibrant after-work life of user group meetings and deep, philosophical discussions on software development methodologies and techniques. I was expecting to find India's Silicon Valley bursting at its seams with an overflow of artisans, enthusiastic in the pursuit of the great craft of software development.

What I found were *a whole lot* of people who were picking up a paycheck and *a few* incredibly passionate craftspeople.

Just like back home.

Of course, I didn't realize it was just like back home at the time. I had a few data points from the United States, but I always assumed I was just working in bad cities or bad company environments. I counted situations like my first experiences with IT employment as outliers. *Most software developers must get it,* I thought. *I just haven't found the right environment yet.*

I started work at my university's IT department on a blind recommendation from my friend Walter, who had seen me work with computers enough to know I could probably make them do things better than most of the people who needed help at the university. I didn't believe I could, having had no formal training. I was just a saxophone player who liked to play video games. But, Walter actually filled out an application for me and set up an interview. I was hired without so much as a single technical question being asked, and I was to start immediately.

When I showed up on the job, I was paranoid I would be discovered as the charlatan I really was. *What is this saxophone player doing here with us trained professionals?* After all, I was working with people who had advanced computer science degrees. And, here I was with only part of a music degree trying to fit in as if I knew something.

Within a few days of work, the truth started to sink in. *These people don't know what the hell they're doing!* In fact, some people were watching me work and *taking notes*! People with *master's degrees in computer science*!

My first reaction was to assume I was surrounded by idiots. After all, I didn't have any formal training. I spent my nights playing in bar bands and my days playing computer games. I had learned how to work with computers only because I was interested in them. In fact, I really learned how to write programs because I wanted to make my own computer games. I would come home late after a deafening evening at a bar and browse Gopher[5] sites with tutorials on programming until the sun came up. Then I'd sleep, wake up, and continue my learning until I had to go out and perform again. I'd break up the study with my beloved computer games, eat, and then go back to goofing around with Gopher and whatever compilers I could get working.

Looking back on it, I was addicted, but in a good way. My drive to create had been ignited in much the same way that it had when I

> **Work because you couldn't *not* work.**

started writing classical music or playing improvisational jazz. I was obsessed with learning anything and everything I could. I wasn't in this for a new career. In fact, many of my musician friends thought of it as an irresponsible distraction from my actual career. I was in it because I couldn't *not be.*

This was the difference between me and my overeducated, underperforming colleagues at work. Passion.

These people had no idea *why* they were in the IT field. They had stumbled into their careers, because they thought computer programming might pay well, because their parents encouraged them, or because they couldn't think of a better major in college. Unfortunately, their performance on the job reflected it.

---

5. Gopher is a document-sharing system similar in intent to the World Wide Web. Its popularity declined dramatically with the rise of the Web.

If you think about the biographies you read or the documentaries you watch about the greats in various fields, this same pattern of addictive, passionate behavior surfaces. Jazz saxophone great John Coltrane reportedly practiced so much that his lips would bleed.

Of course, natural talent plays a big role in ability. We can't all be Mozart or Coltrane. But, we can all take a big step away from mediocrity by finding work we are passionate about.

It might be a technology or business domain that gets you excited. Or, on the other hand, it might be a specific technology or business domain that drags you down. Or a type of organization. Maybe you're meant for small teams or big teams. Or rigid processes. Or agile processes. Whatever the mix, take some time to find yours.

You can fake it for a while, but a lack of passion will catch up with you and your work.

Act on It!

1. Go find a job you're actually passionate about.

2. Starting next Monday, keep two weeks of a simple log. Every workday when you wake up, rate your level of excitement on a scale from 1 to 10—1 means you would rather come down with an actual sickness than go to work, and 10 means you could hardly stay in bed because you were consumed by the idea of getting the next thing done.

    After two weeks of keeping this log, review the results. Were there spikes? Were there trends? Was it all low or all high? What would your average grade be if this were a school test?

    For the next two weeks, every morning plan how you're going to make tomorrow a 10. Plan what you're going to do *today* to make tomorrow one of those workdays you can't wait to start. Each day, log *yesterday's* excitement level. If after two weeks things are looking sad, it might be time to consider a major change.

Being a Serial Opportunist

by James Duncan Davidson

From the word go, I haven't had what many would consider to be a traditional career path. Instead, it's been very much a path of following opportunities as they present themselves. The first of these opportunities presented itself while I was in school working on a degree in architecture. I had decided at age 15 or 16 that I wanted to be an architect, and I spent a lot of time investing in that future. But the seeds of what would actually be my career after school were sown in my early fascination with online BBS systems. I was one of those kids who loved the 300-baud modem in the family PC. That led me eventually to the Internet, which lead me to Gopher and then the World Wide Web.

The Web immediately hooked me. I built several personal websites in quick succession and took advantage of every available technology at my disposal, teaching it all to myself as needed. At the time, I thought of this work as experiments in cyberarchitecture. It sounds overly grandiose and even quite dorky now, but it was the world in which those of us in the early days of the Web were living. We were trying to imagine what the future might bring.

Of course, the real job of building the future of the Internet wasn't happening in architecture labs. It was happening in the world of business. Soon enough, and based on what I had accomplished with my public website, I was contacted by a startup that was building websites for the likes of Hilton and the Better Business Bureau. They had seen the websites I had built, and apparently I had just the skill set they needed. I was offered a job with what seemed at the time a ludicrously great salary. I took it, figuring that I could ride the wave for a while, bank some money, and return to school in a few years.

It was 1995. Little did I have any idea just how far things would go and where a bit of willingness to dig into something new would take me.

While helping to build the first version of the Hilton website that had real-time reservation placement, I learned how to build websites using a variety of server-side technologies. In a few months, I went from apprentice to creating my own server-side frameworks. Looking back, it seems ridiculous, but at the time, it was what was necessary. I saw an opening, took it, and parlayed it for all it was worth, reinventing myself as necessary.

Being a Serial Opportunist (continued)

One thing led to another. In 1997, I went to JavaSoft to work on server-side software, and after a few years, I ended up in charge of the Servlet specification. Unfortunately, it was an underfunded effort, and I didn't have a team to help me do everything that needed to be done, including build a new reference implementation. I didn't let that stop me, however, and set off to build a completely new ground-up implementation that was eventually released as the JavaServer Web Development Kit. Not many people remember that piece of software. But most people who work with Java on the server side knows about the next release of that code. It's called Tomcat. And it was released to the world via the Apache Software Foundation with a sidekick called Ant. The story behind that release would fill a book. Suffice it say that it all happened through a perfect set of opportunities that I was able parlay.

After working at Sun for four years and facing a "What do I do next?" kind of question, I decided to go independent. I wrote books for O'Reilly. I developed software for the Mac. I developed quite a bit of my own software that I didn't end up releasing. And, I ended up doing a bit of Ruby on Rails development. Being an independent software developer was good to me, and I'm pretty good at it. But along the way, a hobby I had been pursuing started to grow into its own career.

In addition to being an architecture student turned technologist, I've long been a photographer. My grandmother taught me the basics. My parents encouraged me. As a result, for as long as I can remember, I've had a camera around. It's been a big part of my life. In fact, the unreleased software I wrote for myself after leaving Sun was for working with photographs.

In 2005, ten years after I got a break and switched gears from architecture student to software developer, I got a call from my friends over in the O'Reilly Conferences group. They needed someone to document their events and asked if I'd be interested in coming out and taking a few snaps. I accepted, but instead of making just a few photographs, I went a bit beyond my brief. I went nuts and worked all the important sessions and posted images to Flickr to provide an extremely quick turnaround. I was invited back and, over the last four years, have built up a business around it with a wide range of clients.

Being a Serial Opportunist (continued)

As I write this, I still hack code from time to time, and I even do a bit of software work for a few clients. But, for the most part, I'm pretty much a full-time photographer these days. That might change, however. You never know. It's hard to say what the future will bring.

What I do know is that I'm a serial opportunist. When I see something interesting and exciting to me, I jump in and do whatever it takes to succeed. Usually this means learning new skills and picking up new capabilities. Some may find it a drag to build new skills up, but for some reason I love learning how to do new things. After all, new skills let you do new things. And I've never defined myself by my skills. Instead, I've always defined myself by what I have done and what I want to do next. Skills are just a way to get there.

James Duncan Davidson is a programmer and photographer.

Part II

Investing in Your Product

I'm not bragging when I say that, as a saxophonist, I am naturally gifted. You'll have to trust me for a minute while I explain how that's a liability. When I was playing saxophone full-time, I played a *lot*. I sometimes had two or three gigs per day when times got really busy. I might find myself playing jazz at a brunch, dance music at an evening wedding, and rhythm and blues at a party or late-night bar all on the same day. And, as a natural on the saxophone, I found myself improving and learning on the job. I had an especially good tone and a natural ability to learn songs by ear and improvise.

But I never really *invested* in myself as a saxophonist. Things came easily enough to me that I guess I was satisfied. I was also typically a go-to guy in the bands I played in, so I didn't feel much pressure from my peers.

I didn't realize it, but I was slowly stagnating. Whereas I made rapid progress when I was younger, the more R&B gigs I played, the more I sounded the same. My tone sounded the same night to night. My improvised solos were rehashed regurgitations of the same thing I'd played the night before—or earlier the same night. It wasn't just me, now that I think of it. It was the entire professional music scene around me. We were not challenging ourselves, and the audience was definitely not challenging us (ever heard an audience clap and cheer because a saxophonist held a note for more than thirty seconds?).

For several years, until recently, I let myself get busy enough with work that I didn't prioritize music at all. This led to a long period of completely neglecting my saxophones and guitars. I realized I missed the influence of music in my life and recently picked both back up in earnest. This time, I have no local musician friends. I have no time to play professionally, nor do I have the dexterity to play well enough. So, I'm just playing for myself.

Maybe it's because I'm older now. Or smarter, but I doubt that. But, this time I've discovered that a little investment goes a *long* way. Instead of just pulling out the instruments and heading for a gig, I've been (necessarily) playing by myself. This has led me to a more focused approach to the instruments. I've been listening to music and making lists of techniques I want to learn. For example, I've always wanted to be able to do a specific thing that Phil Woods always does in alto saxophone solos. Or I've wanted to learn how Prince makes his guitar scream the way he does at the end of "Let's Go Crazy" from the *Purple Rain* album.

It turns out that, coupled with my natural talent, a few hours of investment have made these "always wanted to be able to do it" abilities attainable. And as I've started to put in the investment, it builds on itself. One technique leads to the next, and one barrier-breaking practice session motivates the next.

After a few months of focused intention, I'm in many ways playing better than I ever have, even when I was playing full-time. The structured me who invests in his abilities (even as a hobby) completely wipes the floor with the me who bets it all on natural talent and ability.

This is one piece of proof that if you want to have a great *product* to sell on the job market—a product that stands out and that lets you really compete—you're going to have to invest in that product. In business, ideas and even talent are a dime a dozen. It's the blood, sweat, tears, and money you pour into a product that make it really *worth something*.

In this part, we'll look at investment strategies for your career. We will explore how to choose which skills and technologies to invest in as well as look at different *ways* of investing in ourselves. This part is where the real work starts.

Learn to Fish

Lao Tzu said, "Give a man a fish; feed him for a day. Teach a man to fish; feed him for a lifetime." That's all well and good. But Lao Tzu left out the part where the man doesn't want to learn how to fish and he asks you for another fish tomorrow. Education requires both a teacher and a student. Many of us are too often reluctant to be a student.

Don't wait to be told. Ask! Just what is a *fish* in the software industry? It's the process of using a tool or some facet of a technology or a specific piece of information from a business domain you're working in. It's how to check out a specific branch from your team's source control system, or it's getting an application server up and running for development. Too many of us take these details for granted. *Someone else can take care of this for me*, you may think. The build guy knows about the source control system. You just ask him to set things up for you when you need them. The infrastructure team knows how the firewalls between you and your customers are set up, so if you have an application need, you just send an e-mail and the team will take care of it.

Who wants to be at the mercy of someone else? Or, worse: if you were looking to hire someone to do a job for you, would you want that person to be at the mercy of *the experts*? I wouldn't. I'd want to hire someone who is self-sufficient.

The most obvious place to start is in learning the tools of your trade. Source control, for example, is a powerful tool. An important part of its job is focused on making developers more productive. It's not just the place where you put your code when you're done with it, and you shouldn't treat it as such. It's an integral part of your development process. Don't let such an important thing—the authoritative repository of your work—be like voodoo to you. A self-sufficient developer can easily check differences between the version of a project that he or she has checked out and the last known good one in the repository. Or perhaps you need to pull out the last released code and make a bug fix. If your code has a critical bug in the middle of the night, you don't want to have to call someone else to ask them to get you the right version so you can start troubleshooting. This goes for IDEs, operating systems, and pretty much every piece of infrastructure your code or process rides on top of.

Equally important is the technology platform you are employing. For example, you may be developing applications using J2EE. You know you have to create various classes, interfaces, and deployment descriptors. Do you know *why*? Do you know how these things are used? When you start up a J2EE container, what actually happens? You may not be an application server developer, but knowing how this stuff works enables you to develop solid code for a platform and to troubleshoot when something goes wrong.

A particularly easy way to get lazy is to use a lot of wizards that generate code for you. This is particularly prevalent in the world of Windows development where, to Microsoft's credit, the development tools make a lot of tasks really easy. The downside is that many Windows developers have no idea how their code really works. The work of the wizards remains a magical mystery. Don't get me wrong—code generation used correctly can be a useful tool. For example, code generators are what translate high-level C# code to byte codes that can run on the .NET runtime. You obviously wouldn't want to have to write all those byte codes yourself. But, especially at the higher levels, letting the wizards have their way leaves your knowledge shallow and leaves you limited to what the wizards can already do for you.

We may easily overlook the fish in our business domain. If you're working for a mortgage company, either you could ask an expert for the calculation of an interest rate for each scenario that you need during testing or you could learn how to calculate it yourself. Although interactions with your customer are good and it's good to clarify business requirements with them (as opposed to half-understanding and filling in the details yourself), imagine how much faster you could go if you actually knew the ins and outs of the business domain you're working in. You probably won't know every single business rule—that's not your job. But, you can at least learn the basics. Many of the best software people I've worked with over the years have become more expert in their domains than even some of their business clients. This results in better products. Someone who is domain-ignorant will let silly mistakes slip through—mistakes that a basic knowledge of the business domain would have avoided. Furthermore, they'll go slower (and ultimately cost the company more) than the equivalent developer who understands the business.

For us software developers, Lao Tzu's intent might be equally well served with "Ask for a fish; eat for a day. Ask someone to teach you to fish; eat for a lifetime." Better yet, don't *ask* to be taught—go learn for yourself.

Act on It!

1. *How and why?*—Either as you sit here reading or the next time you're at work, think about the facets of your job that you may not fully understand. You can ask yourself two extremely useful questions about any given area to drill down into the murky layers: *How does it work?* and *Why does this (have to) happen?*

   You may not even be able to answer the questions, but the act of asking them will put you in a new frame of mind and will generate a higher level of awareness about your work environment. *How does the IIS server pass requests to my ASP.NET pages? Why do I have to generate these interfaces and deployment descriptors for my EJB applications? How does my compiler deal with dynamic vs. static linking? Why do we calculate tax differently if a shopper lives in Montana?*

   Of course, the answer to any of these questions will lead to another potential opportunity to ask the question again. When you can't go any further down the *how and why* tree, you've probably gone far enough.

2. *Tip time*—Pick one of the most critical but neglected tools in your toolbox to focus on. Perhaps it's your version control system, perhaps a library that you use extensively but you've looked into only superficially, or maybe the editor you use when programming.

   When you've picked the tool, allot yourself a small period of time each day to learn *one new thing* about the tool that will make you more productive or put you in better control over your development environment. You may, for example, choose to master the GNU Bourne Again Shell (bash). During one of those times when your mind starts to wander from the task at hand, instead of loading up Slashdot, you could search the Internet for *bash tips*. Within a minute or two, you should find *something* useful that you didn't know about how to use the shell. Of course, now that you have a new trick, you can dive into its guts with a series of *Hows* and *Whys*.

Learn How Businesses Really Work

In the previous chapter, we discussed the importance of making an intentional choice about the business domain in which you work. Domain knowledge, being at best an employment differentiator for a job and at worst a showstopper, isn't something you should take lightly. Before making an investment in learning the ins and outs of a business domain, you should make sure you're investing in the right one for you and for the state of the market.

But, one body of knowledge is neither technical nor domain-specific and won't be outdated at any time soon: the basics of business finance. Regardless of your line of business, whether it be manufacturing, health care, nonprofit, or an educational institution, it is still a *business*. And, *business* is itself a domain of knowledge that one can—indeed, must—learn.

I remember as a young programmer going to staff meetings, my eyes glazing over as some big-shot leader with whom I would never directly work showed chart after chart of numbers that I believed to be completely irrelevant to me. *I just want to go back and finish the application feature I'm working on,* I would whine to myself. My teammates sat together, looking like a row of squirming children on a long car ride. None of us understood what was being presented, and none of us cared. We blamed what we felt was a complete waste of time on the incompetent managers who had called the meeting.

Looking back on it, I realize how foolish we were. We worked for a business, and our job was to contribute to either making or saving money for that business. Yet we

> You can't creatively help a business until you know how it works.

didn't understand the basics of how the business came to profitability. Worse, we didn't think we needed to know. We were programmers and system administrators. We thought our jobs were strictly about those topics that we had devoted ourselves to. However, how were we supposed to *creatively* help the business be profitable if we didn't even understand how the business *worked*?

The use of the word *creatively* in the previous paragraph is the key. It's plausible to have the view that we are indeed IT specialists and that is what we are paid to be. Given the right projects and leadership, we should be putting effort into tasks that help the business. We don't need to fully understand how a business runs to provide value to it.

But, to *creatively* add value takes a more thorough understanding of the business environment in which you work. In the business world, we hear the phrase *bottom line* all the time. How many of us truly understand what the bottom line is and what contributes to it? More important, how many of us really understand how *we* contribute to the bottom line? Is your organization a cost center or a profit center (do you add to or take away from the bottom line)?

Understanding the financial drivers—and language—of your company will give you the ability to make meaningful changes, rather than stabbing in the dark at things that seem intuitively right to you.

Act on It!

1. Go get a book on basic business, and work through it. A trick for finding a good overview book is to look for books about getting a master's of business administration (MBA) degree. One such book that I found particularly useful (and pleasantly short) is *The Ten-Day MBA: A Step-By-step Guide To Mastering The Skills Taught In America's Top Business Schools* [Sil99]. You can actually get through it in ten days. That's not a very big investment.

2. Ask someone to walk you through the financials of your company or division and explain them to you (if this is information your company doesn't mind sharing with its employees).

3. Explain them back.

4. Find out why the bottom line is called *the bottom line*.

Find a Mentor

One thing the jazz music culture has really gotten right is the practice of mentorship. It's common in the jazz world for young musicians to find more experienced musicians who will take them under their wings and pass down the lineage of the jazz tradition. It doesn't stop there, though. These older musicians often serve as career counselors, life advisors, and sounding boards. In exchange, the younger musicians are fiercely loyal, building up a support and rabid fan network around their mentors.

Connections are made and players are hired every day via these relationships. The society of jazz culture has created a self-organizing culture and set of customs around the mentor/mentee relationship. It's a system that works so well that you would suspect it was guided by some kind of organizing body.

In the traditional professional world (and specifically the IT trade), we're less likely to ask each other for help. Depending on others is often seen as a sign of weakness.

> It's OK to depend on someone. Just make sure it's the right person.

We're afraid to admit that we're not perfect. Everything is competition. Only the strong survive, and all that. Unfortunately, this leads to an extremely underdeveloped system of mentoring. If I were to ask a handful of jazz musicians, "Who is your mentor?" most of them would have an answer. Now ask the same question of programmers. In the United States, they'd probably respond with "What?"

It hasn't always been like this here. The history of the West includes a thriving system of professional mentoring, extending back into the Middle Ages. The craftsmanship approach to professional training was even stronger and more formalized than the system that has evolved in the music scene. Young people would start their professional careers as apprentices to respected master craftsmen. They would work in exchange for a nominal salary and the privilege of learning from the master. The master's obligation was to train the apprentices to create things in the tradition (and of the quality) of the master himself.

The first and most important purpose that a mentor serves is that of a role model. It's hard to know what's possible until you see someone who can stretch the limits you're familiar with. A role model sets the standard for what "good" means. If you thought of yourself as a chess player, for example, just being able to beat the people in your immediate family might feel pretty good. But, if you played with a tournament player, you would find that chess is a much deeper game than you ever knew. If you were to play with a grand master, you'd have another such revelation. If you keep playing with, and beating, your immediate family members, you might get the idea that you're *really good* at chess. Without a role model, there's no incentive to get better.

A mentor can also give structure to your learning process. As you saw in the previous chapter, you have an overwhelming number of choices to make about which technologies and domains to invest in. Sometimes, too many choices can get you stuck. Within reason, it's better to be moving in one direction than to be sitting still. A mentor can help take some of the choice out of what to focus your energies on.

When I started my career as a system support person, I latched onto a saint named Ken who was one of our university's network administrators. He came in to bail me out of a big problem with our campus NetWare network that was crippling the students who were trying to use our computer labs, and after that point, he was unable to shake me (nor did he try). When I prodded him to give me direction on how to become more knowledgeable and self-sufficient, he gave me a simple recipe: dive into directory services, get comfortable with a UNIX variant, and master a scripting language.

He picked three skills for me to learn from the infinite number available. And, with the confidence that this person, who I considered to be a master, had prescribed them, I set out to learn those three skills. My career since has been built on the foundation of those pieces of knowledge, all three of which are still completely relevant in everything I do. It's not that Ken's direction was the absolute right answer—there are no absolute right answers. The important thing is that he narrowed down the long list of skills I *could* be learning into the short list of skills I *learned*.

A mentor also serves as a trusted party who can observe and judge your decisions and your progress. If you're a programmer, you can show them your code and get pointers. If you're planning to give a presentation at the office or a local user group meeting, you can run it by your mentor beforehand for feedback. A mentor is someone you can trust enough to ask, "What should be different about me as a professional?" because you know that they'll not only criticize you but they'll help you improve.

Finally, just as in jazz music, not only do you create a personal attachment and responsibility to your mentor, but the reverse happens as well. If my role in a relationship is to help someone, I become invested in that person's success. I'm nudging someone along their career on a path that I believe is the right one. So, if that path leads to success, it's my success as well.

This creates incentive on the part of the mentor for his or her mentees to succeed. Typically, being more experienced and already successful, a person in such a role would have the respect of a significant network of people. The mentor becomes a positively reinforced connection from you to his or her network. The importance of this kind of connection can't be underestimated. After all, the phrase "It's not what you know. It's who you know" isn't a cliche for nothing.

The degree of formality in a mentor relationship is not important. Nobody has to explicitly ask someone to be their mentor (though it's definitely not a bad thing if you do). In fact, your mentor may not even *know* they are serving that role for you. What's important is that you have someone you trust and admire that can help give you career guidance and help you hone your craft.

Act on It!

1. *Mentoring yourself*—We'd all ideally have someone to actively mentor us, but the reality is that we won't always be able to find someone in the same location that we can place in this role. Here's a way to proxy-mentor yourself.

    Think of the person in your field whom you admire most. Most of us have a short list already formulated from some stage in our careers. It may be someone we've worked with, or it may be someone whose work we admire. List the ten most important attributes of this role model. Choose the attributes that are the reason why you have chosen this person to be your role model. These attributes might be specific areas of skill, such as technology breadth, or the depth of their knowledge in some particular domain. Or, they might be more personal traits like the ability to make team members comfortable or that they are an engaging speaker.

Now, rank those qualities in order of importance, with 1 being the least important and 10 being the most important. You have now created and distilled a list of attributes that you find admirable and important. These are the ways in which you should strive to emulate your chosen role model. But, how do you choose which to focus on first?

Add a column to the list, and for each item on the list, imagine how your role model would rate *you* on a scale of 1 to 10 (10 being the best). Try to really put yourself into the mind of your role model and to observe yourself as if a third person.

When you have the attributes, ranking, and your own ratings, in a final column subtract your rating in each row from the importance level you gave it in the preceding column. If you ranked something as 10, the most important attribute of your role model, and your rating was 3, that gives you a final priority score of 7. Having filled this column in completely, sorting in descending order will you give a prioritized top ten list of areas in which you need to improve.

Start with the top two or three items, and put together a concrete list of tasks you can *start doing now* to improve yourself.

Be a Mentor

If you want to really learn something, try teaching it to someone else. There's no better way to crystallize your understanding of something than to force yourself to express it to someone else so that *they* can understand it. The simple act of speaking is a known elixir for treating an unclear mind. Speaking to puppets and other inanimate objects as a method of problem solving is a fairly well-known element of software development folklore.

I saw Martin Fowler[6] give a talk to a room of developers in Bangalore, in which he said that whenever he wants to really learn about something, he writes about it. Martin Fowler is a well-known software

> To find out whether you really know something, try teaching it to someone else.

developer and author. It could be said that he is one of the best-known and influential *teachers* this industry has to offer if we consider his role as author to be that of a remote teacher and mentor.

We learn by teaching. It's ironic, because we expect a teacher to already know things. Of course, I don't mean we can learn new facts altogether by teaching them to someone—where would they come from? But, knowing facts is not the same as understanding their causes and ramifications. It's this kind of deeper understanding that we develop by teaching others. We look for analogies to express complex concepts, and we internally work through the reasons why one analogy seems to work but doesn't and another analogy would seem not to work but does. When you teach, you have to answer questions that may have never occurred to you. Through teaching, we clean the dusty corners of our knowledge as they are exposed to us.

So, just as you can benefit from finding a mentor, you can benefit from *being* a mentor to someone else.

---

6. No, we're not related.

Mentoring has positive social effects as well. An overlapping group of mentors and their mentees creates a tight and powerful social network. The mentor-to-mentee bond is a strong one, so the links in this kind of professional network are stronger than those of more passive acquaintances. When you are in a mentoring relationship with someone, you form an allegiance with each other. A network of this kind is a great place to circulate difficult problems or look for work.

> **Mentors tend not to get laid off.**

You also shouldn't underestimate that it just *feels good* to help people. If you can hold the interests of others in mind, you will have actually done something altruistic with your skills. In the uncertainty of today's economic environment, actually *helping* someone is a job you can't be laid off from. And, it pays in a currency that doesn't depreciate with inflation.

You find a mentee not by going out and declaring yourself a guru but by being knowledgeable and willing to patiently share that knowledge. Don't be alarmed if you're not an absolute expert on a topic. Chances are that there is *something* that you have experience with that would qualify you to help someone less experienced. Find that thing, and start being helpful.

You might, for example, have done a sizable amount of PHP work. You could go to your local PHP user group meeting and offer to help less experienced users with their specific problems. Or, if you don't have an immediately available forum for providing face-to-face mentoring, you could simply start answering questions in an online message board or IRC channel or help people debug application problems. Keep in mind, though, that mentoring is about people. An online mentoring relationship can never compare to one that happens between two humans in the same place.

You don't have to set up a formal mentoring relationship to get these benefits. Just start helping people, and the rest will come naturally.

Act on It!

1. Look for someone to take under your wing. You might find someone younger and less experienced at your company, perhaps an intern. Or, you could talk to the computer science or information systems

department at your local university and volunteer to mentor a college student.

2. Find an online forum, and pick a topic. Start helping. Become known for your desire and ability to patiently help people learn.

Practice, Practice, Practice

When I was a music student, I spent long nights in my university's music building. Through the thin walls of the university's practice rooms, I was constantly immersed in some of the ugliest musical sounds imaginable. It's not that the musicians at my school weren't any good. Quite the contrary. But they were practicing.

When you practice music, it *shouldn't* sound good. If you always sound good during practice sessions, it means you're not stretching your limits. That's what practice is for. The same is true in sports. Athletes push themselves to the limit during workouts so they can *expand* those limits for the real performances. They let the ugliness happen behind closed doors—not when they're actually working.

In the computer industry, it's common to find developers stretched to their limits. Unfortunately, this is usually a case of a developer being underqualified for the tasks that he or she has undertaken. Our industry tends to practice on the job. Can you imagine a professional musician getting onstage and replicating the gibberish from my university's practice rooms? It wouldn't be tolerated. Musicians are paid to *perform* in public—not to practice. Similarly, a martial artist or boxer stressing himself or herself to fatigue during matches wouldn't go very far in the sport.

As an industry, we need to make time for practice. We in the West often make the case for domestic programmers based on the relatively high quality of the code they produce vs. that of offshore teams. If we're going to try to compete based on quality, we have to stop treating our jobs as a practice session. We have to *invest the time* in our craft.

Several years back, I started experimenting with programming exercises modeled after my musical practice sessions. Rule number one was that the software I was developing couldn't be something I wanted to use. I didn't want to cut corners, rushing to an end goal. So, I wrote software that wasn't useful.

I cut no corners but was frustrated to find that a lot of the ideas I had while practicing weren't working. Though I was trying to do as good a job as possible, the designs and code I was creating weren't as elegant as I had hoped they'd be.

Looking back on it now, I see that the awkward feeling I got from these experiences was a *good sign*. My code wasn't completely devoid of brilliant moments. But I was stretching my mental muscles and building my coding chops. Just like playing the saxophone, if I sat down to practice and nothing but pretty sounds came out, I'd know I wasn't practicing. Likewise, if I sit down to practice coding and nothing but elegant code comes out, I'm probably sitting somewhere near the *center* of my current capabilities instead of the edges, where a good practice session should place me.

So, how do you know what to practice? What stretches your limits? The subject of how to practice

Practice at your limits.

as a software developer could easily fill a book of its own. As a start, I'll borrow again from my experience as a jazz musician. I'd break jazz practice down into the following categories (simplified for the nonmusicians among us):

- Physical/coordination
- Sight reading
- Improvisation

These might serve as a framework for *one way* to think about practice as a software developer.

Physical/coordination: Musicians have to practice the technical aspects of their instruments: sound production, physical coordination (making your fingers move nimbly, for example), speed, and accuracy are all important to practice.

What equivalent do we software developers have of these musical fundamentals? What about the dusty corners of your primary programming language that you rarely visit? For example, does your programming language of choice support regular expressions? Regular expressions are an extremely powerful and tragically underutilized feature of many programming environments. Very often developers don't use them when they could, because they don't have the level of skill that it would take to be productive with them. As a result, a lot of needless string-parsing code gets created and then has to be maintained.

The same rules apply to your language's APIs or function libraries. If you don't get the environment's many tools under your fingers (as musicians say), it's less likely you'll pull them out when they could really help you. Try truly digging into, for example, the way multithreaded programming works in your chosen programming environment. Or, how about stream libraries, network programming APIs, or even the set of utilities available for dealing with collections or lists? Most modern programming languages offer rich and powerful libraries in all of these areas, but software developers tend to learn a small subset, with which they can less efficiently write the same code they could have written if they had mastered the full set of tools available to them.

Sight reading: Especially as a studio musician, the ability to read and play music near perfectly the first time is paramount for a professional. I once played saxophone on a jingle for Blockbuster (the video rental company). I played both the lead and second alto parts on an up-tempo big-band song. I saw the music for the first time literally as the tape started rolling. We played through once on the lead part and once on the second part. Any mistakes, and the whole band had to do it again—and the cost of the studio time had to be accounted for.

As software developers, what would it mean to be able to sight read code? Or requirements specifications or designs? An excellent place to find new code with which to practice is the open source community. Do you have any favorite pieces of open source software? How about trying to add a feature? Go look at the to-do list for a piece of software you'd like to practice with, and give yourself a constrained amount of time to implement the new feature (or at least to determine what it would take to implement it).

After choosing a feature, download the source code for the software, and start exploring. How do you know where to look? What tricks do you use to find your way around a significant body of code? What's your starting place?

This is an exercise you can practice often and in short periods of time. You don't actually *have* to implement the feature. Just use it as a starting point. The real goal is to understand what you're looking at as quickly as possible. Be sure to vary the software you work with. Try different types of software in different styles and languages. Take note of issues that make it easier or harder for you to find your way around. What patterns are you developing that help you work through the code? What virtual bread crumbs do you leave for yourself to help you navigate as you move up and down the call stack of a complex piece of functionality?

Improvisation: Improvisation is taking some structure or constraint and creating something new, on the fly, on top of that structure. As a programmer, I've found myself doing the most improvisation in times of stress. *Oh no! The wireless network app server is down, and we're losing orders!* That's when some of the most creative, impromptu programming happens. That's when you do crazy stuff like recovering lost data by manually replaying packets over a wireless network from a binary log file. Nobody meant for you to do these things, especially not in the heat of the moment. That kind of sharp and quick programming ability can be like a magical power when wielded at the right time.

A great way to sharpen the mind and improve your improvisational coding skills is to practice with self-imposed constraints. Pick a simple program, and try to write it with these constraints. My favorite exercise is to write a program that prints the lyrics to the tired old song "99 Bottles of Beer on the Wall." How could you write such a program without doing any variable assignments? Or, how small of a program can you write that will still print the lyrics correctly? For an additional constraint, how *fast* can you code this program? How about practicing small, difficult problems with a timer?

This is just one limited perspective on how to practice. You can mine examples from any discipline, from visual arts to monastic religious practice. The important thing is to find *your* practice needs and to make sure you're not practicing during your performances (on the job). *You* have to make time for practice. It's *your* responsibility.

Act on It!

1. *TopCoder*—TopCoder.com is a long-standing programming competition site. You can register for an account and compete online for prizes. Even if you're not interested in competing with others, Top-Coder offers a practice room with a large collection of practice problems that you can use as excellent fodder for your practice sessions. Go sign up, and give it a try.

2. *Code Kata*—Dave Thomas, one of the Pragmatic Programmers (our beloved publisher), took the idea of coding practice and made

something…well, pragmatic out of it. He created a series of what he calls *Code Kata*, which are small, thought-provoking exercises that programmers can do in the language of their choice. Each kata emphasizes a specific technique or thought process, providing a concrete flexing of one's mental muscles.

At the time of this printing, Dave has created twenty-one such kata and has made them available for free on his weblog (http://codekata. pragprog.com/). On the weblog, you'll also find links to a mailing list and to others' solutions to the exercises along with discussion about how the problems were solved.

Your challenge: work through all twenty-one kata. Keep a diary (perhaps a weblog?) of your experiences with the kata. When you've finished working through all twenty-one exercises, write your *own* kata, and share it with others.

The Way That You Do It

"Developing software" is not a thing, a noun. Instead, "developing software" is a *verb phrase*; it's the *process* of creating a thing. When we're coding away, it's as important to focus on the process we're using as it is to focus on the product being developed. Take your eye off the process, and you risk delivering late, delivering the wrong product, or not delivering at all. These outcomes tend to be frowned on by our customers.

Fortunately, a lot of thought has been put into the process of making good software (and products in general). Much of this prior art has been codified into a group of *methodologies*. These methodologies are the subject of numerous books that can be found online or in your local bookstore.

Unfortunately, most developers don't get to benefit from all this good information. For the majority of teams, the process is an afterthought or something imposed from above. The word *methodology* has, in their minds, become synonymous with paperwork and long, meaningless meetings. All too often, a methodology is something that their managers impose.

Managers intuitively know that they need to follow *some kind of* process, but they often don't know about the options that are now available. As a result, they dust off the same processes that were imposed on them in the 1980s, wrap them up in buzzword-compliant ribbons (the pastel-colored Agile ribbon is a good choice at the moment), and pass the practices on to their teams. And unless someone breaks the cycle by actually doing research on what works and what doesn't, the same process will happen again as the developers on the team become managers themselves.

You'd think that there must be a better way to develop software. And for most teams there is.

If you're a programmer, tester, or software designer, you may not think the development process is your responsibility. As far as your company is concerned, you're probably right. Unfortunately, it's usually *nobody's* responsibility. If it does get assigned to someone, it might fall into the hole of a "process group" or some other similarly disconnected organization. The truth is that for a software process to have any chance of being implemented successfully, it has to be embraced by the people who are using the process—people like you.

The best way to feel ownership of processes is to help implement them. If your organization has no process, research methodologies that might work for you. Have brown-bag lunches with your team to discuss current development problems and ways that adopting a standard process might mitigate them. Put together a plan for rolling the chosen process into your organization, and get everyone's buy-in. Then start to implement your plan.

> If you want to feel you own a process, help implement it.

Alternatively, you might work in an environment where a process is passed down from on high. By the time the tablets arrive at the development team, the practices have often been watered down and reinterpreted to the point where they're unrecognizable from the originals. The process has suffered the same fate as the secret phrase in a game of Chinese Whispers.[7] Again, this is an opportunity to take the initiative. Research the methodology you've been given, and help interpret what it really means, both to your team and to your management. You're not going to be able to fight that a process has been imposed, so you may as well make it work by doing it right.

The methodology world can quickly begin to sound like a hollow shell of buzzwords. But, as buzzword compliant as some may be, you can always learn *something* from the study of a software process—even if that something is what *not* to do. If you're well versed in the software process landscape, you can make a more credible argument for how your team should be working.

Even with the abundance of prescriptive methodologies to choose from, it's not likely you will ever work for a company that fully implements any of them. That's OK. The best process to follow is the one that makes your team most productive and results in the best products.

---

7.   http://en.wikipedia.org/wiki/Chinese_whispers

Methodologies: Not Just for Geeks

Though project management is not necessarily bound to software development methodology, you may find yourself running face first into your company's project management techniques. Numerous project management methodologies are in use throughout the industry. Probably most notable is the Project Management Institute's *Project Management Book of Knowledge*,[a] (with its widely recognized certification program).

Six Sigma[b] is another non-software-specific quality methodology. Driven by companies such as General Electric and Motorola, the Six Sigma approach emphasizes the measurement and analysis of processes and products to drive customer satisfaction and efficiency. Although not specific to software development, Six Sigma's rigorous and methodical approach offers many lessons that are directly applicable to your job as a programmer.

---

a.   http://www.pmi.org/
b.   http://www.isixsigma.com/

The only way to find that hybrid (short of revelationary epiphany) is to study the available options, pick out the pieces that make sense to you and your team, and continuously refine them based on real experience.

Ultimately, if you can't do the process, you can't do the product. It's much easier to find someone who can make software work than it is to find someone who can make the *making of* software work. So, adding knowledge of the software development process to your arsenal can only help you.

Act on It!

1.   Pick a software development methodology, and pick up a book, start reading websites, and join a mailing list. Look at the methodology with a critical eye. What do you think would be its strong and weak points? What would be the barriers to implementing it where you work? Next, do the same with another. Contrast their strengths and weaknesses. How could you combine their approaches?

On the Shoulders of Giants

As a jazz musician, I spent a lot of time listening to music. I didn't just play music in the background while I was reading or driving. I would really *listen* to the music. If jazz improvisation is all about playing what you hear over the chords of a song, then actually listening to music is a critical source of inspiration and knowledge of what works and what doesn't. What sounds great and what just sits there.

The vast history of jazz recordings serves as an incredible body of knowledge, there for the taking by anyone with the skill to hear it. Listening to music, therefore, is not a passive activity for a jazz musician. It is study. Furthermore, the ability to understand what you're hearing is a skill that you develop over time. My circle of musician friends actually did this kind of listening explicitly. We would have listening parties, where a bunch of jazz musician geeks would sit around listening to music and then discussing it. Sometimes we would play *name that improviser* where one of us would play a recording of an improvised solo and the rest of us would have to figure out, based on style, who the recorded improviser was.

We in the jazz world weren't special, of course. Classical composers do the same thing. So do novelists and poets. So do sculptors and painters. Studying the work of masters is an essential part of becoming a master.

When listening to jazz recordings, we would discuss the musical devices that improvisers would use to communicate their musical points. "Wow! Did you hear the way he started sidestepping at the end of the form?" or "That was really strange the way he was playing behind the beat on the bridge." These discussions would help us all distill and discover tricks that we could take with us to our next improvisation session to try.

Mine existing code for insights.

Software design and programming have a lot in common with the arts in this way. We can mine a huge body of existing code for patterns and tricks. The design patterns movement (see *Design Patterns: Elements of Reusable Object-Oriented Software* [GHJV95]) is focused on the discovery and documentation of reusable solutions to common software development problems. Design patterns have formalized the study of existing code, making the practice accessible to a great number of software professionals. Still, design patterns address only a small subset of the kinds of learning we can enjoy through code reading.

How do other programmers solve particular problems algorithmically? How do others strategically use variable, function, and structure naming? If I wanted to implement the Jabber instant messaging protocol in a new language, how might I do it? What creative ways can I find to handle interprocess communication between UNIX and Windows systems? These are the type of questions you can answer through the study of existing code.

Even more important than finding solutions to specific problems is the use of existing code as a magnifying mirror to inspect our own

> Use existing code to reflect on your own capabilities.

style and capabilities. Just as listening to a John Coltrane recording always reminded me of where I stood on the skill ladder as a saxophonist, reading the work of a *great* software developer has a similarly humbling effect. Nevertheless, it's not just about being humbled. As you're reading through code, you will find things that you would have never done. You will find things you might have never even thought of. Why? What was the developer thinking? What were his or her motivations? You can even learn from bad code with this kind of critical, self-aware exploration of an existing work.

The act of learning from the work that came before you works well in the arts world, because there is no hidden source code for a painting or a piece of music. If you can hear the music or see the piece of art, you can learn from it. Thankfully, as software developers we have access to a practically infinite array of existing software in the form of open source software.

Enough open source software is available that it would be impossible to ever actually read all of it. There are definitely some bad open source projects, but there are also quite a few *great* ones. There is open source code available implementing almost any task that can be done with software in almost every available programming language.

As you look at this code with a critical eye, you will start to develop your own tastes, just as you would for music, art, or literature. Various styles and devices will amuse you, amaze you, anger you, and (I hope) *challenge* you. If you're really looking for them, you'll find everything from tricks that make you more productive to design paradigms that completely change the way you approach a class of problems. Just as in the arts, by studying and learning from the habits of others you will develop your own distinctive style of software development.

A positive side effect of reading code is that you will learn more about what already exists. When you have a new problem that needs solving, you might remember that "Oh, I saw a library that implements MIME type handling in such and such project." If the licensing terms are right, you may save yourself a lot of time and your company a lot of money by becoming more aware of what's already out there for the taking. You might be amazed to realize just how much money we waste in the software industry by reimplementing the wheel (*invention* would be too generous a word) over and over again.

Sir Isaac Newton said, "If I have seen further, it is by standing on the shoulders of giants." Smart guys like Isaac know that there is much to be learned from those who came before us. Be like Isaac.

Act on It!

1. Pick a project, and read it like a book. Make notes. Outline the good and the bad. Write a critique, and publish it. Find at least one trick or pattern that you can use from it. Find at least one bad thing that you observed that you will add to your "What not to do" checklist when you're developing software.

2. Find a group of like-minded people, and meet once a month. Each session have someone nominate some code to study—2 lines to 200 lines. Break it down. Discuss what's behind it. Think of the decisions that went into it. Ponder the code that *isn't* there.

Automate Yourself into a Job

A constant theme of my career has been the conflict between IT management's desire to engage low-cost (often offshore) consulting companies to do project work and my strong belief that the cheapest developer doesn't usually lead to the lowest cost. I've had many a fiery conversation with an IT director or vice president, passionately arguing to hire a few really strong developers instead of a legion of low-cost, low-skill coders.

Unfortunately, I've often been shut down midargument. The problem with my position isn't that I'm wrong (obviously!). It's that there's no easy way to prove that I'm right. And, from a cost perspective, the only hard evidence we have leads to the conclusion that a lower per-hour cost is indeed advantageous to the company doing the hiring.

Imagine a hypothetical software project of whatever scope your mind comes up with. How many programmers does it take to write a piece of software like this in three months? Five, you say? Six? (Bear with me for a moment.) OK, how about the same project in two months? How do you shave a month off?

The standard IT management answer is that you add programmers to go faster. It's wrong, but that's what people believe. And, if you can make a single project go faster by adding programmers, the extrapolation of this rule is that more people means more productivity.

There's more than one way to skin that cat. If the goal is to enhance software development throughput, you can

- get faster people to do the work,
- get *more* people to do the work, or
- automate the work.

Since we don't yet know how to truly measure software development productivity, it's hard to prove that one person is faster than another. So, finance managers focus on per-hour costs.

This leads to this simple (minded) formula, which assumes a fixed period of time:

$$\text{Productivity} = \frac{\text{Number of Projects}}{\text{Number of Programmers} \times \text{Hourly Rate}}$$

In some environments, it's actually possible to calculate the true yield of a software investment. In most, you'll find squishy, amorphous measures such as *number of projects* or *number of requirements,* with no repeatable way of measuring one of those units.

So, the *faster programmer* approach is too hard to prove, and we *don't want to encourage* the *add more cheap programmers* approach. This leaves us with automation.

I remember the sensationalism surrounding job loss in the United States in the 1980s. Back then, not only were we blaming other countries, but we were blaming machines and, specifically, computers. Huge robotic arms were being installed in manufacturing plants. These robotic arms could outperform humans in both throughput and accuracy to a point that it was not even worth comparing them. Everyone was upset—everyone, that is, except for the people who *created* the robotic arms.

So, imagine your company is in the business of creating websites for small businesses. You basically need to create the same site over and over again, with contacts, surveys, shopping carts, the works. You could either hire a small number of really fast programmers to build the sites for you, hire an army of low-cost programmers to do the whole thing manually and repetitively, or create a system for *generating* the sites.

If we plug some (made-up) numbers into our finance manager's formula, we get the equations shown in Figure 1, *Productivity comparisons,* on page 72.

Automation is part of the DNA of our industry. Yet for some reason we don't tend to automate *our* work as software developers. How can you *provably* make better software faster and cheaper than your offshore competition? Make the robots. Automate yourself into a job.

Fast Programmers

$$\frac{5}{3 \times \$80} = 0.02$$

Cheap Programmers

$$\frac{5}{20 \times \$12} = 0.02$$

One Programmer + Robotic Arm

$$\frac{5}{1 \times \$80} = 0.06$$

Figure 1—Productivity comparisons

Act on It!

1. Pick a task you normally do repetitively, and write a code generator for it. Start simple. Don't worry about reusability. Just make sure your generator saves you time.

    Think of a way to raise the level of abstraction of what you are generating.

2. Research model-driven architecture (MDA). Try some of the available tools. Look for somewhere in your work to apply the *concepts* of MDA if not the full toolset. Think about applying MDA concepts with just the tools you use every day.

From IT Consultant to Managing Director

by Vik Chadha

My journey from being an IT consultant at GE to serving as the en-trepreneur-in-residence at bCatalyst (a business accelerator with a $5 million fund) was not a path that I had envisioned as the next step in my career.

So, how did I make the transition from working for a Fortune 5 company with tens of thousands of employees to working for a firm that invested in and mentored early-stage high-tech startups? When I look back and attempt to connect the dots, some important patterns emerged, and I'd like to share them with you with the hope that you can adapt them to your context.

Soon after finishing my master's degree in electrical and computer engi-neering at Virginia Tech, I joined GE as an IT consultant. Commercial use of the Internet was beginning to hit its stride, and I worked on several projects that were designed to make the most of this incredibly powerful platform and its underlying technologies, moving in quick succession from the finance IT team to the technology and services group to sales force automation and finally to the sales data warehousing group, working with each team to develop new initiatives. I loved researching, and then implementing, the latest Internet technologies and applying them to solve difficult business problems.

Living on the bleeding edge of technology was not always fun. We invari-ably ran into problems with technologies that were not yet ready for prime time, and we spent a lot of time and energy helping our vendors debug their products. From a customer's perspective, I learned that no matter how cool the technology seemed to be, it was valuable only if it solved a real problem that was urgent and provided quantifiable benefits. Over time, this helped me change my way of thinking from being tech-nology-centric to being solution-centric. Becoming more self-aware of this new way of thinking proved to be very valuable while evaluating early-stage technology startups at bCatalyst a few years later.

However, as much as I enjoyed working at GE, one important aspect was missing. I felt that in my job as an IT professional, I was primarily develop-ing all my skills in a single dimension and did not have the opportunity to really understand how companies operate, how they make money, what makes them sustainable, and how they innovate. Rather than be-coming frustrated, I decided to take the initiative and do something about it by learning more about business and entrepreneurship.

From IT Consultant to Managing Director (continued)

I had never taken any courses in business and knew that the only way that I was going to learn the ins-and-outs of what it takes to start a company was by getting my hands dirty (that is, learning by doing through trial and error).

An entrepreneurial ex-roommate of mine who was also a very close friend (Raj Hajela), my wife (Vidya), and I brainstormed ideas trying to figure out where there were existing unmet needs in the market. We wanted to explore e-commerce opportunities but did not want to sell anything that was a commodity product. We had a real interest and background in art and liked the fact that every piece of art was unique in nature. My uncle was a lifelong artist who had struggled to make a living. We did some research and concluded that this was the case with most artists. We then decided to solve this problem by creating a platform to help artists publicize and promote their works and keep in touch with their patrons. With this mission in mind, we launched Passion4Art.com and began the hard work of getting artists to join our website and put their digital images of their paintings online. After we had signed up our first 1,000 artists and they had set up their own websites, we believed that we were providing something of value and started looking for outside funding.

At that time (circa 1999), a company called eMazing.com provided daily tips on a variety of topics, and we thought that we could partner with them (by working with our artists and their distribution channel) to provide an Art Tip of the Day. One of their senior executives met with us, liked what we had to offer, and agreed to a trial.

We told him that we were seeking funding in order to build out our infrastructure, and he kindly offered to send our business plan over to a new business accelerator in town called bCatalyst.

A few days later, we received a call from Keith Williams, the CEO of bCatalyst, informing us that they would like to meet us in person and learn more about our venture. We were naturally very excited about this meeting. I did not realize until much later how important it was that they heard about us from a trusted source. The lesson here is that if you ever need to get in touch with a venture capitalist, work hard on getting a warm referral since it is the best way to get one's foot in the door.

Over the course of several meetings with Keith, we realized that there was a good chemistry between our team and theirs, but the Internet bubble had recently burst, and the timing was not good for them to make an investment in this space. At our final meeting, they informed us that they really liked our team but could not justify making an investment.

From IT Consultant to Managing Director (continued)

However, they told us that if we brought them another idea that they liked, they would not hesitate to back us. I asked them if this was a polite way of saying "no" or if they were serious about working with us. They assured us that they meant what they said.

I then requested another meeting with Keith and told him that I was willing to quit GE to work with them full-time over the next few months and jointly explore other startup opportunities. I positioned this as a low-risk proposition for them by not asking them for a long-term commitment (analogous to a try-before-you-buy program). This opportunity materialized because I was able to convince them that I was willing to put my own skin in the game by taking the leap from GE without a clear road map ahead of me.

Over the next twelve months, every day we would meet different teams pitching their ideas to us, and I noticed a new pattern in the set of questions that we asked each company.

I have compiled this list and am sharing the questions with you in case you ever need to raise money from VCs in the future; see http://www.enterprisecorp.com/resources/assessment.htm).

The skills that I picked up during that year at bCatalyst led me to my current job as the managing director of Enterprise Corp. Over the past seven years, I have worked with more than 100 companies and helped them raise more than $75 million in funding. This has been a deeply satisfying experience that wouldn't have been possible if I had not taken the initiative and been adventurous in trying out new things. The many zigs and zags along the way were an integral part of the process. My hope is that you, the reader, will use my story to inspire you to find your own unique path, one that will use your abilities to the fullest.

Vik Chadha is the managing director at Enterprise Corp.

Part III

Executing

You have been making all the right investments and in the right market. You are becoming, for example, an expert in implementing service-oriented architectures for wirelessly enabled pizza delivery applications, and the pizza delivery industry is starting to boom like it has never boomed before. Before getting too wrapped up in amore with yourself, I should warn you that everything we've talked about so far is prep work. It all leads to this moment, where the sauce hits the dough: you have to actually *do something*.

Unless you're really lucky, you're probably not getting paid to be smart. And you aren't getting paid to be a leading expert in the latest technologies. You work for an institution that is, most likely, trying to make money. Your job is to do *something* that helps the organization meet that goal. All of this careful thought and preparation has made you ready to show up at work and start kicking ass for your company.

Like the "I want to be a J2EE architect" guy from Tip 9, *Don't Put All Your Eggs in Someone Else's Basket*, on page 35, most of us don't find our identities in our associations with the companies we work for. I mean, I'm a programmer before I'm a person who helps a Fortune 500 company sell dishwashers, right? I'm an application architect—not a power company employee. From the perspective of viewing software as craft, this is not too surprising. The craft we've chosen isn't usually coupled with the domain in which we're applying that craft. An architect designing an office for a defense contractor is still an architect—not a defense contractor.

This identity observation creates some subtle problems, because our macro-goals may conflict with our micro-responsibilities. If the architect creates an office that is dysfunctional for the defense contractor, he hasn't created something of value. Regardless of the aesthetic beauty of his creation, he's a bad architect.

We're being paid to create value. This means getting up out of our reading chairs and getting things done. To be successful, raw ability will get you only so far. The final stretch is populated by *closers*—people who finish things.

Getting things done feels *good*. It's often hard for people to get into a rhythm (try searching Amazon for *procrastination*), but once you've felt a fire under you, you won't want to stop. Let's start lighting the fire.

Right Now

Imagine you are in a race with a $100,000 cash prize. The first team that creates software to implement a new accounts receivable application wins the prize. You and your team at work have signed up to compete. The contest is to take place over a weekend. To win, your code has to be fully tested and implement a minimum set of specified features. You start on Saturday morning, and you have until Monday morning to complete the application. The first team to finish before Monday morning wins the race. If no team finishes before Monday, the team with the most features implemented wins.

You confidently peruse the application's feature requirements. Looking at the feature set, you realize that the system to be created is similar in size and scope to a lot of systems you've worked on in the past. While your team's agreed-upon goal is to finish some time midday on Sunday, for a fleeting moment you start to question yourself. *How is it that an application of similar scope to those we spend weeks working on in the office is going to get finished in a single weekend?*

But as the opening bell sounds and you launch into coding, you realize that your team *is* going to be able to meet its goal. The team is collectively in a groove, churning out feature after feature, fixing bugs, making split-second design decisions, and getting things done. It feels good. At design reviews and status meetings in the office, you've often daydreamed about taking a small team out of the bureaucratic environment and ripping through the creation of a new application in record time.

Many of us have this daydream. We *know* that our processes slow us down. Not only that, but we know that the speed of our environments cause *us* to slow down.

What can we do? Right now?

Parkinson's law states that "Work expands so as to fill the time available for its completion." The sad thing is that even when you don't want it to be this way, you can fall into the trap, especially when there are tasks you don't really want to do.

In the case of a weekend coding race, you don't have time to put tasks off, so you don't. You can't delay making a decision, so you don't. You can't avoid the boring work, and you know that you have to do it so quickly that nothing can get *too* boring.

Parkinson's law is an empirical observation—not an unescapable human mandate. A sense of urgency, even if manufactured, is enough to easily double or triple your productivity. Try it, and you'll see. You can do it faster. You can do it now. You can get it done instead of talking about getting it done.

If you treat your projects like a race, you'll get to the end a lot faster than if you treat them like a prison cell. Create movement. Be the one who pushes. Don't get comfortable.

Always be the one to ask, "But what can we do *right now*?"

Act on It!

1. Look at your proverbial plate. Examine the tasks that have been sitting on it for a long time, the projects that are starting to grow mold, or the ones you've been just a little bit *stuck* on—perhaps in bureaucracy, perhaps in analysis paralysis.

    Find one that you could just *do* in between the cracks of your normal work, when you would normally be browsing the Web, checking your e-mail, or taking a long lunch. Turn a multimonth project into a less-than-one-week task.

Mind Reader

I used to work with this guy named Rao. Rao was from a state in southern India called Andhra Pradesh, but he was located in the United States and worked onsite with us. Rao was the kind of guy who could code anything you asked him to code. If you needed low-level system programming done, he was the guy to ask. If you needed high-level application programming, he could do pretty much anything you asked him to do.

However, what made Rao truly remarkable was what he did *before* you asked him. He had this uncanny ability to predict what you were going to ask him to do and do it before you thought of it. It was like magic. I believe I even accused him of playing tricks on me at one point, but there's no way it could have been a trick. I would say, "Rao, I've been thinking about changing the way we're encapsulating the controller on our application framework. If we changed it just a tad, it could be used for applications other than web applications. What do you think?"

"I did that earlier this week," he would say. "It's checked into version control. Have a look." This was *constantly* happening with Rao. It happened so often that the only way it could have been a coincidence is if Rao was literally doing *everything imaginable* with every piece of software that our team maintained.

At the time, I was leading my company's application architecture team. Among other things, we built and maintained frameworks for use in the company's applications. My teammates spent a lot of time talking about how we wanted to see the face of software development at the company improve. We also talked a lot about the role of our core infrastructure components in these improvements.

That's where Rao's magic trick came in. He didn't talk much in those conversations, but he was anything but disengaged. He was listening carefully. And, giving away his secret as no magician would, he later told me the trick was that he was only doing things that I had already said I wanted. I had just said them in ways that were subtle enough that *even I* didn't realize I had said them.

We might be standing around waiting for a pot of coffee to brew, and I would talk about how great it would be if we had some new flexibility in our code that didn't exist before. If I said it often enough or with enough conviction, even though I hadn't really put it on the team's to-do list, Rao might fill the gaps between "real work" looking at the feasibility of implementing one of these things. If it was easy (and cheap) to implement, he'd whip it out and check it in.

Mind reading not only applies to your managers but also to your customers. If they're giving you the right cues, you might be able to add features that they're either

> The mind-reading trick, if done well, leads to people depending on you.

going to ask for or *would have* asked for if they had realized they were possible. If you always do what your customers ask for when they ask for them, you will satisfy your customers. However, if you do *more* than what they ask for or you have already done things before they ask, you will delight them—that is, unless your ability to read minds is defective.

This mind-reading trick isn't entirely safe. It's a tight rope that you'll want to avoid walking unless you have left yourself a safety net. The major risks (with some suggested mitigations) are as follows:

- You spend the company's money doing work that nobody asked you to do. What if you were wrong? Start small. Only do the guesswork that you can fit in between the cracks of your normal job so the impact is little to none. If you're so inclined, take on these extra jobs in your free time.

- Any time you add code to a system, you stand the very strong chance of making it less resilient to change. Avoid mind-reading work that may force the system down a particular architectural path or limit what the system can do in some way. When the impact of change is great enough, a business decision needs to be made. And, it's seldom just the developers who need to weigh in on such a decision.

- You might take it upon yourself to change a feature your customers *did* ask for in a way that, unexpectedly to you, makes it less functional or desirable to the customer. Beware of guessing when it comes to user interfaces especially.

Managing people and projects is challenging work. People who can keep a project moving in the right direction without being given much guidance are highly valued and appreciated by their often overworked managers and customers. The mind-reading trick, if done well, leads to people depending on you—an excellent recipe for a career you can drive the direction of. It's a skill worth exploring and developing.

Act on It!

1. An early reviewer for this book, Karl Brophey suggests that for your next project or a system you maintain, start making some notes about what you *think* your users and managers are going to ask for. Be creative. Try to see the system from their points of view. After you have a list of the not-so-obvious features that might come up, think about how you could most effectively implement each feature. Think about edge cases that your users might not immediately have in mind.

    As you get into the project or enhancement requests, track your hit rate. How many of your guesses turned out to be features you were actually asked to implement? When your guessed features *did* come up, were you able to use the ideas you came up with in your brainstorming session?

Daily Hit

We all like to believe, by virtue of our knowledge and that we're good software people, that we are going to naturally nail execution and be top performers. For a lucky few (and I *do* mean to use the word *luck* here), a strategy like this will work.

But, all of us can benefit from scheduling and tracking our accomplishments. Common sense tells us that if we exceed our managers' expectations, we'll be on the A list. Given that exceeding expectations is a worthy goal, surprisingly few of us have mechanisms of tracking how and when we exceed the expectations of our employers.

As with most tasks that are worth doing, becoming a standout performer is more likely with some specific and intentional work. When was the last time you went above and beyond the call of duty? Did your manager know about it? How can you increase the *visible* instances of this behavior?

James McMurry, a co-worker who is also a good friend,[10] told me very early in both of our careers about a system he had worked up

> Have an accomplishment to report every day.

to make sure he was doing a good job. It struck me as being remarkably insightful given his level of experience (maybe it's a hint he got from his parents), and I use it to this day. Without warning his manager, he started tracking *daily hits*. His goal was to, each day, have some kind of outstanding accomplishment to report to his manager—some idea he had thought of or implemented that would make his department better (Figure 2, *One week of hits*, on page 87).

Simply setting a goal (daily, weekly, or whatever you're capable of) and tracking this type of accomplishment can radically change your behavior. When you start to search for outstanding accomplishments, you naturally go through the process of evaluating and prioritizing your activities based on the business value of what you might work on.

---

10. http://www.semanticnoise.com

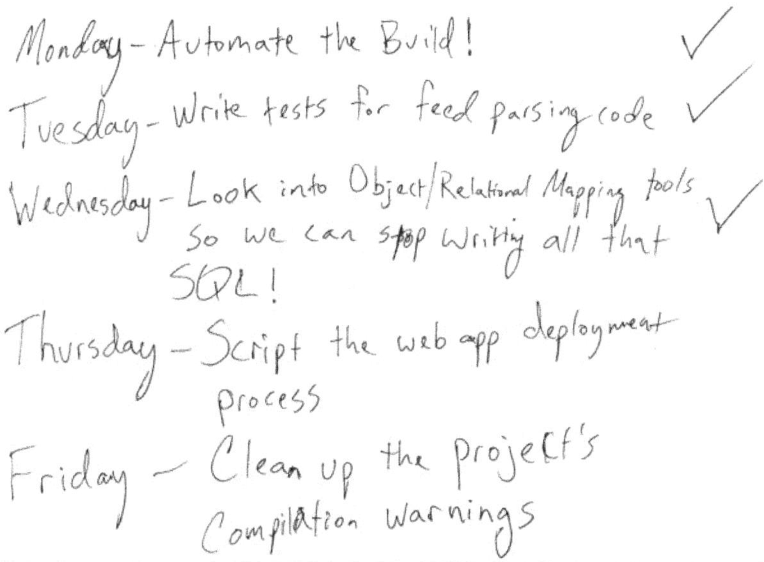

Figure 2—One week of hits

Tracking hits at a reasonably high frequency will ensure that you don't get stuck: if you're supposed to produce a hit per day, you can't spend two weeks crafting the *perfect* task. This type of thinking and work becomes a habit rather than a major production. And, like a developer addicted to the green bar of a unit test suite, you start to get itchy if you haven't knocked out today's hit. You don't have to worry so much about tracking your progress, because performing at this level becomes more akin to a nervous tic than a set of tasks that need to be planned out in Microsoft Project.

Act on It!

1. Block off half an hour on your calendar, and sit down with a pencil and paper in a quiet place where you won't be interrupted. Think about the little nitpicky problems your team puts up with on a daily basis. Write them down. What are the annoying tasks that waste a few minutes of the team's time each day but nobody has had the time or energy to do anything about?

   Where in your current project are you doing something manually that could be automated? Write it down. How about your build or deployment process? Anything you could clean up? How might you reduce failures in your build? Write all of these ideas down.

Give yourself a solid twenty minutes of this. Write down all of your ideas—good or bad. Don't allow yourself to quit until the twenty minutes are up. After you've made your list, on a new sheet of paper write out your five favorite (most annoying) items. Next week, on Monday, take the first item from the list, and do something about it. On Tuesday, take the second item, Wednesday the third, and so on.

Remember Who You Work For

It's really easy to say "Make sure your goals and your work align with the goals of your business." It's really easy to say; it's really hard to do, especially when you're a programmer buried under so many organizational layers that you hardly know what your business is. Early in my career, I worked for a major package delivery company in a software development architecture team that supported the company's revenue systems. This company was so encumbered with hierarchy, I never saw anything in my daily work that gave me even a glimpse into the business of package delivery. I can remember my team attending quarterly all-hands meetings and feeling completely disjointed and alienated. "What is this achievement we're celebrating? What do all of these metrics mean?"

Granted, at that point in my career, I was more interested in building elegant systems and hacking open source software than digging into the guts of a package delivery business. (OK, I admit it—I'm *still* more interested in those things.) But, had I really wanted to align my work with the major goals of the organization, I'm not sure I would have known where to begin.

So, it's all fine and dandy to say we need to align our work with the goals of the company—to try to make sure we're impacting the bottom line and all that. However, truth be told, many of us just don't have visibility into how we can do this at the level from which we're grasping. We can't see the forest for the trees.

Maybe this one isn't our fault. We may be asking too much of ourselves. Maybe the idea of trying to directly impact the company's bottom line feels a bit like trying to boil the ocean. So, we need to take a more compartmentalized view, breaking the business into boilable puddles.

The most obvious puddle to start with is your own team. It's probably small and focused enough that you can conceptually wrap yourself around it. You most likely understand the problems the team faces. You know what your team is focused on improving, whether it's productivity, revenue, error reduction, or anything else. If you're not sure, you have one obvious place to go to find out: your manager.

Ultimately, in a well-structured environment, the goals of your manager are the goals of your team. Solve your manager's problem, and you've solved a problem for the team. Additionally, if your manager is taking the same approach you are, the problems you're solving for him or her are really his or her boss's problems. And so on, and so on, until it rolls up to the highest level of your company or organization—the CEO, the shareholders, or even your customers.

By doing your small part, you're contributing to the fulfillment of the goals of your company. This can give you a sense of purpose. It gives your work meaning.

Some may resist this strategy. "I'm not going to do his work for him." Or, "She's just going to take credit for my work!"

Well, yeah. Sort of. That's the way it works. The role of a good manager is not to, as Lister and DeMarco say in *Peopleware: Productive Projects and Teams* [DL99], "play pinch hitter," knowing how to do his or her whole team's job and filling in when things get difficult. The role of a good manager is to set priorities for the team, make sure the team has what it needs to get the job done, and do what it takes to keep the team motivated and productive, ultimately getting done what needs to get done. A job well done by the team is a job well done by the manager.

If the manager's job is to know and set priorities but not to personally *do* all the work, then your job *is* to do all the work. You are not doing the manager's job for him or her. You're doing your job.

> Your managers' successes are *your* successes.

If you're really worried about who gets the credit, remember that it's your *manager* who holds the keys to your career (in your present company, at least). In most organizations, it's the direct manager who influences performance appraisals, salary actions, bonuses, and promotions. So, the credit you seek is ultimately cashed in with your manager.

Remember who you work for. You'll not only align yourself with the needs of the business, but you'll align the business with *your* needs. If you're going to *nail* the execution of your job, this will ensure that you're executing on the right things.

Act on It!

1. Schedule a meeting with your manager. The agenda is for you to understand your manager's goals for the team over the coming month, quarter, and year. Ask how you can make a difference. After the meeting, examine how your daily work aligns to the goals of your team. Let them be a filter for everything you do. Prioritize your work based on these goals.

Be Where You're At

As a manager, I can tell you that the most frustrating thing to deal with is an employee who's always aiming for the next rung on the ladder. You know the guy: you can't sit with him for lunch without him bringing up who got what promotion. He always has some kind of office gossip to spread, and he seems to cling to corporate politics as if clinging to the story line of a soap opera to which he has some sick and sinful addiction. He complains about the incompetence of The Management and bitterly completes his tasks, knowing full well that he could do the job of management better than they can. They're just too incompetent to understand his potential.

He thinks many tasks are beneath him. He avoids them when possible and does them begrudgingly (and slowly) when not. He cherry-picks work that he thinks, even if subconsciously, is in tune with his level and might get him closer to his goal of the next promotion.

The sad thing about this guy is that, because he's living in the next job, he's usually doing a mediocre job in his current role. It's like

> Be ambitious, but don't wear it on your sleeve.

mowing the lawn for me. I hate mowing the lawn. It makes me itch, and it makes me sweat. Worst of all, it keeps me from doing something I'd *rather* be doing. You can hire people to mow the lawn. I've been one of those people. That was a long time ago, and now I've graduated. So, when I *have* to mow the lawn, what do I do? I rush. I do a sloppy job. I spend the whole time thinking about how to get it finished so I can get on to the stuff I'd rather be doing. In a nutshell, I do a terrible job at mowing the lawn.

Thankfully, in my lawn-mowing example, nobody is watching what I'm doing and grading me on it (though, my wife has become sufficiently annoyed that I'm not responsible for the lawn at our house anymore). It's my own problem if the lawn doesn't look great when I've finished. Nobody is holding me back to being "just a lawn mower" because of my performance in the yard. In the case of an IT job, that very same behavior could bring on a career catastrophe.

Going back to our friend from the previous paragraphs, how do you think his management is going to view him? Will they see that they've been wrong to overlook his brilliance and decide to promote him? Will they give him big raises to try to make him happy?

Of course not. He's a mediocre performer with a bad attitude. *So what* if he has high potential! Right now, he's not showing it. The company doesn't make money because of potential. Shareholders don't hang onto investments if their potential isn't met. Furthermore, his attitude makes his managers want to stop investing in *him*.

So, that's a manager's viewpoint. Now, of course, I'm not completely guilt-free here. I've been this guy myself to some extent. It really isn't very good from this side of the street either. You spend all your time wanting something. Craving is the opposite of contentment. You wake up in the morning and have to go to "that bloody job" where nobody understands your potential. With resentment, you toil over your work, going over strategies for how to get ahead. You fantasize about what *you* would do in the latest situation that your manager screwed up—how you would handle it differently. You put off living while you're at work until you can do it *your* way in the position you deserve.

Here's a secret: that feeling will never end. If and when you finally land the big promotion you've been dreaming about, you'll quickly grow tired and realize that it's not *this* job you were meant for—it's the *next* one. The cycle begins again. I haven't reached the top yet, but I have a strong hunch that if there were such a position and I were to reach it, I would look ahead and realize I'd been chasing a ghost. What a frustrating waste of a professional life.

But, shouldn't we have ambitions? Would there be a Microsoft or a General Electric if the great entrepreneurs hadn't been ambitious and had goals?

Of course we should. I'm not advocating an apathetic outlook. It's good to have goals, and it's good to want to succeed. But, think of the negative, resentful guy I described at the beginning of this section. Do you think that guy is going to be the one who succeeds? It seems backward, but keeping your mind focused on the present will get you further toward your goals than keeping your mind focused on the goal itself.

It sounds difficult at first. Monk-like, even. Casting off the daily drive to succeed may sound like an ascetic, unattainable goal. You'll find that it's very pragmatic, though. Focusing on the present allows you to enjoy the small victories of daily work life: the feeling of a job well done, the feeling of being pulled in as an expert on a critical business problem, the feeling of being an integral member of a team that *gels*. These are what you'll miss if you're always walking around with your head in the clouds. You'll always be waiting for *the big one* while ignoring the little things that happen every day that make your job worth showing up for.

Not only will *you* feel better, but those around you will feel it as well. Your co-workers, managers, and customers will feel it. It will show in your work. As unintuitive as it may be, letting go of your desire to succeed will result in an enhanced *ability* to succeed.

You are close to your clients. You are close to the leaders and decision makers who will shape your career in the short term and, possibly, the long term. Developers in India or the Philippines don't have this advantage, but *you* do. So, *be* where you're *at*.

Act on It!

1. Put your career goals away for a week. Write down your goals for your *current* job. Instead of thinking about where you want to go next, think about what you want to have accomplished when you finish the job you're in. What can you have *produced* in this job that will be great? Create a plan that is both strategic and tactical. Spend the week implementing these tactics in support of the long-term goal of "finishing" this job.

   During lunches and breaks with your co-workers, focus the conversation on these goals. Steer yourself and those around you away from any conversation about career advancement or office politics and gossip.

   At the end of the week, take stock of your progress toward meeting these job goals. How long will it be before you've accomplished everything you feel you need to in your current role? How will you know you're done? Plan the next week and repeat.

How Good a Job Can I Do Today?

It's rewarding to do a good job and to be appreciated. Although most of us know this intuitively, we allow ourselves to be extremely selective about where and when we really go out of our way to excel. We dote over the design for the marketing department's Next Big Thing project, or we're quick to jump in to save the day in the face of some big, visible catastrophe, because our brains are wired to understand these moments as opportunities to show our proverbial stuff. We'll even do our work in the middle of the night with a level of focus and detail that would normally bore us to tears. A dire situation will often bring out the best in us.

I've let that intoxicating feeling of elation keep me awake and working effectively through some of the most grueling system outages and missed deadlines. Why is it that, without facing great pressure, we're often unable to work ourselves into this kind of altruistic, ultra-productive frenzy? How well would you perform if you could treat the most uninteresting and annoying tasks with the same feverish desire to do them right?

> How much more *fun* could you make your job?

That last question may be better if we restate it. How much more *fun* would your job be if you could treat the most uninteresting and annoying tasks with the same feverish desire to do them right? When we have more fun, we do better work. So, when we have no interest in a task, we're bored, and our work suffers as a result.

How can you make the boring work more fun? The answer to that question might be more apparent if you flip it around. Why is the boring work boring? Why isn't it *already* fun? What's the difference between the work you enjoy and the work you abhor?

For most of us techies, the boring work is boring for two primary reasons. The work we love lets us flex our creative muscles. Software development is a creative act, and many of us are drawn to it for this reason. The work we *don't* like is seldom work that we consider to be creative in nature. Think about it for a moment. Think about what you have on your to-do list for the next week at work. The tasks that you'd love to let slip are probably not tasks that leave much to the imagination. They're just-do-'em tasks that you wish you could just get someone else to do.

The second reason that the boring tasks are boring, admittedly closely joined to the first, is that the boring tasks are not challenging. We love to dig in and solve a hard problem where others have failed. It's the same feeling that drives members of our species to recreationally risk their lives scaling mountains and bungee jumping off bridges. We love to do things to prove that we're able. The boring tasks are usually no-brainers. Doing them is about as challenging as taking out the trash.

So, how can we still use our creativity and challenge ourselves while tending to the mundane leftovers of our workday (which probably take up greater than 80 percent of the time for most of us)?

What if you tried to do the boring stuff *perfectly*? Say, for example, you hate unit testing. You love programming, but you get annoyed with having to write automated test code. What if you strove to make your tests perfect? How might that change your behavior? What does *perfect* even mean with regard to unit testing? It probably has something to do with test coverage. Perfect test coverage would mean that you had tested 100 percent of the functionality of your real code. Perfect unit tests are also clean and maintainable and don't depend on a lot of external factors that might be hard to replicate on another computer. They should be runnable directly after a fresh version control checkout on a new machine. And, of course, all of the tests should pass at 100 percent.

This is starting to sound difficult; 100 percent test coverage almost sounds impossible. And the business of decoupling the tests so that they can run without external dependencies presents a lot of challenges. In fact, you'll probably have to change your code to make this even possible. But, if you could do it, the tests would be incredible.

I don't know about you, but that sounds kind of fun to me. Granted, this is a manufactured example, but you can apply the same type of thinking to most of the tasks that cross your path. Try it tomorrow. Look at your workday and ask yourself, "How good a job can I do today?" You'll find that you'll like your job better, and your job will like you.[11]

Act on It!

1. *Make it visible*—Turn those boring tasks into a competition with your co-workers. See who can do them better. Don't like writing unit tests? Print out the number of test assertions for the code you checked in every day, and hang it on your cubicle walls. Keep a scoreboard for the whole team. Compete for bragging rights (or even prizes). At the end of a project, arrange for the winner to have his or her grunt work done by the rest of the team for a whole week.

---

11. Thanks to Andy Hunt for this idea (http://blog.toolshed. com/2003/07/how_good_a_job_.html).

How Much Are You Worth?

Have you ever stopped to consider exactly how much you cost to the company you work for? I mean, you know your salary. That part is easy. What about benefits, management overhead, training, and all that other stuff that doesn't necessarily show up on your paycheck?

It's easy to get into the mode of just *wanting more*. It unfortunately seems to be a basic human tendency, in fact. You get a salary increase, and it feels good for a little while, but then you're thinking about the next one. "If I could make just 10 percent more, I could afford that new…." We've all done it. At some point, the actual number becomes abstract. It's not about $5,000 more per year. It's about making whatever the baseline number is go up. If we don't get a satisfactory salary increase one year, we become dissatisfied with our work and our company. "Why don't they appreciate me?"

How much do you really cost? As I already mentioned, it's obviously more than your base salary. For the sake of discussion, let's estimate it at roughly two times your base salary. So, if you make $60k per year, the company actually spends about $120k keeping you employed.

That was easy. Now's the hard part: how much value did you produce last year? What was your *positive* impact on the company's bottom line? We already know that you cost the company (in our imaginary scenario) roughly $120k. What did you give back? How much money did you cause the company to save? How much more in revenues did you contribute?

Is that number bigger than twice your salary?

It's a difficult exercise to go through, because it's often hard to relate every aspect of our work to the bottom line of the company. It may even seem like an unreasonable question to you. "How do I know? I'm just a coder!" That, of course, is the point. You work for a business, and unless you provide some kind of real value, you are a waste of money. It's easy to fall into the trap of thinking that salary increases are an entitlement. Analogously, a company has the right to charge more for its products every year. But, consumers have the right to *not purchase that product* if the price isn't attractive.

Now that you've started thinking about how much you cost vs. how much you deliver, how much do you think you need to deliver to be considered a worthwhile investment to the company? We've talked about the rough twice-your-salary figure, but is that enough? If you deliver value totaling twice your salary, the company has broken even. Is that a good way to spend money?

As a point of reference, think about the interest rate on a typical consumer savings account. It's not great, right? Still, it's definitely better than zero. Given the choice, would you put a year's worth of savings into a savings account that yields 0 percent or 3 percent? To deliver only twice your salary in value is as unappealing a prospect for a company as a 0 percent savings account is to you. They've tied up $120k in cash for the year, and you're not even delivering enough value to keep up with the economy's inflation rate. Breaking even in this case is actually still a loss.

I can remember when I started thinking this way. It made me paranoid at first. A month would pass, and I would think, "What did I deliver this month?" Then, I started getting as granular as weeks and days. "Was I worth it today?"

Ask, "Was I worth it today?"

You can make this concrete. Just how much value *do* you add? Talk to your manager about how to best quantify it. The very fact that you *want* to quantify it will be taken as a good thing. How could you creatively save the company money? How could you make your development team more efficient? Or what about the end users of your software? You'll be surprised at how many opportunities you can spot if you start asking these questions. Now, start implementing some of them. Hold that figure in your head: *twice my salary*. Don't let yourself off the hook until you've surpassed that number for the year.

Act on It!

1. When companies make investments, they try to make sure they're using their money in the best possible way. Simply calculating a return on investment (I put in $100 and get back $120) isn't enough to make a smart decision. Among other factors, companies have to take inflation, opportunity cost, and risk into consideration.

Specifically unintuitive to those of us who haven't been to business school is the concept of the time value of money. At risk of oversimplification, it goes something like this: a dollar today is worth more than a dollar next year, because a dollar today can be used to *generate more dollars*.

Most companies set a *rate of return* bar, under which an investment will not be made. Investments have to yield an agreed-upon percentage in an agreed-upon period of time, or they aren't made. This number is called the *hurdle rate*.

Find out what your company's hurdle rate is, and apply it to your salary. Are you a good investment?

A Pebble in a Bucket of Water

What would happen if you got up and walked out of your office, never to return? I know a lot of programmers who take comfort in imagining that scene. You just stand up, walk to your boss's office, and hand in your resignation. *I'll show them why they needed me!* This works as a daydream to get you through the really bad days, but it's obviously not a very productive attitude to carry with you all the time.

Beside that, it's not true. People leave companies every day. Many of them are let go. Many choose to leave. Some even live out your daydream and walk out with no notice. But in few cases do the companies they leave actually feel a significant impact as a result of their departure. In most cases, even in critical positions, the effect is surprisingly low. Your presence on the job is, to the company, like a pebble in a bucket of water. Sure, the water level is higher as a result. You get things done. You do your part. But, if you take the pebble out of the bucket and stand back to look at the water, you can't really see a difference.

I'm not trying to depress you. We all need to feel that our contributions mean something. And, they do. But, we spend so much time being *me* that we can easily forget that everyone else is a *me*, too. Everyone employed at your company walks around, a sentient and autonomous being, stuck in this thing called a *self*, which is the only window from which they see their jobs. Think of it this way: if you left tomorrow, the difference would be (on the average) no more or less impactful than if any of your co-workers left.

I once worked for a CIO who was one of the most powerful CIOs in one of the most powerful companies in the world. He and his team (of which I was a part) were winning every award and setting every IT standard in the company. This was a guy who had obviously figured out some kind of magic elixir and was sprinkling it into the free lunches and dinners that he had served during Y2K parties.

One of the few real pieces of advice that I ever got from this CIO—and I heard it over and over again—is that you should never get too comfortable. He professed to waking up every day and intentionally and explicitly reminding himself that he could be knocked off of his pedestal any day. *Today could be it,* he'd say.

His staff would look at him incredulously. No. Today couldn't be it. Things are going so well. You've got too much going for you.

That was his point. Humility is not just something we develop so we can claim to be more spiritual. It also allows you to see your own

> Beware of being blinded by your own success.

actions more clearly. What our CIO was teaching us was that the *more successful* you are, the more likely you are to make a fatal mistake. When you've got everything going for you, you're less likely to question your own judgment. When the way you've always done it has always worked, you're less likely to recognize a new way that might work better. You become arrogant, and with arrogance you develop blind spots. The less replaceable you *think* you are, the more replaceable you are (and the less desirable you become).

Feeling irreplaceable is a bad sign, especially as a software developer. If you can't be replaced, it probably means you perform tasks in such a way that others can't also do them. Although we'd all like to claim some kind of special genius, few software developers are so peerless that they in fact *should* be irreplaceable.

I've heard lots of programmers half-joking about creating "job security" with unmaintainable code. And, I've seen actual programmers attempt to do it. In every case, these people have become *targets*. Sure, it was scary for the company to finally let go of them. Ultimately, though, fear is the worst that ever came of it. Attempting to be irreplaceable is a defensive maneuver that creates a hostile relationship with your employer (and your co-workers) where one may not have already existed.

Using this same logic, attempting to be *replaceable* should create an unhostile working relationship. We're all replaceable. Those of us who embrace and even work toward this actually differentiate ourselves and, unintuitively, improve our own chances. And, of course, if you are replaceable, nothing is stopping you from moving *up* to the next big job.

Act on It!

1. Inventory the code you have written or you maintain along with all the tasks you perform. Make a note of anything for which the team is completely dependent on you. Maybe you're the only one who fully understands your application's deployment process. Or there is a section of code you've written that is especially difficult for the rest of the team to understand.

    Each of these items goes on your to-do list. Document, automate, or refactor each piece of code or task so that it could be easily understood by anyone on your team. Do this until you've depleted your original list. Proactively share these documents with your team and your leader. Make sure the documents are stored somewhere so that they will remain easily accessible to the team.

    Repeat this exercise periodically.

Learn to Love Maintenance

Several years ago, I was involved in setting up a 250-person software development center from scratch. We started with an empty building and were tasked with hiring and filling out an entire development organization. In setting up this development center, we faced a challenge we never expected. Everyone wanted to make new systems. Nobody wanted to maintain old systems. We wanted to create a new environment with an energized culture, so we had to pay attention to what our new employees *wanted* if we were going to start off on the right path.

Everyone likes creating. That's when we feel we are given the opportunity to really put our stamps on a piece of work. To feel like we own it. To express ourselves through our creation. We also tend to believe project work is the most visible to our organizations. The people who build the new generation are the ones who must get the glory, right? I knew this attitude to be prevalent from the previous programmers I had worked with. But, in dealing with a couple hundred software developers in what amounted to a human resources petri dish, I saw this to an extreme that I never expected.

Though software developers are typically creative, freedom-loving people, the programmer "society" is surprisingly caste-like. Programmers want to be designers, who want to be architects, and so on. Maintenance work gives them neither a notch in their belts nor a clear, elevated role (such as *architect*) that they can tell their parents or college buddies.

So, the motivating factors are the ability to be creative and the chance to make steps toward a promotion. The funny thing about it is that project work is *not* necessarily the best place to do either.

Maintenance work is typically littered with old, rotting systems and pushy end users. Since the software is thought of as being done, IT departments are usually focused on reducing the cost of maintaining these systems, so they look for the cheapest possible way to keep the systems running.

That usually amounts to too few resources being assigned to look after the systems and no significant investment dollars being pumped into rejuvenating the systems.

Project work, on the other hand, is where you start with a nice, clean, green field. In a well-run company, every project contributes to either making or saving money, so the projects are usually funded sufficiently for the work to be done (though, experiences may vary here). There is no existing minefield of old code that the programmers have to tiptoe carefully through so they can develop features "right" with fewer hindrances than if they were working on an existing system. In short, the circumstances in project land are usually much more ideal.

If I give you $1,000 and ask you to go get me a cup of coffee, I'm going to be very unhappy if you return with 1,000 less dollars and no cup of coffee. I'm even going to be unhappy if you bring me plenty of really nice coffee but it takes you two hours. If I give you $0 and ask you to go get me a cup of coffee, I'll be extremely appreciative if you actually return with the coffee, and I'll be understanding if you don't. Project work is like the first scenario. Maintenance is like the second.

When we don't have the constraints of bad legacy code and lack of funding to deal with, our managers and customers rightfully expect more from us. And, in project work, there is an expected business improvement. If we don't deliver it, we have failed. Since our companies are counting on these business improvements, they will often put tight reins on what gets created, how, and by when. Suddenly, our creative playground starts to feel more like a military operation—our every move dictated from above.

> Maintenance can be a place of freedom and creativity.

But in maintenance mode, all we're expected to do is keep the software running smoothly and for as little money as possible. Nobody expects anything flashy from the maintenance crew. Typically, if all is going well, customers will stay pretty hands-off with the daily management of the maintainers and their work. Fix bugs, implement small feature requests, and keep it running. That's all you have to do.

What if a bug turns up the need to redesign a subsystem in the application? That's all part of bug fixing, right? The designs may be old and moldy, and broken windows[12] may be scattered throughout the system. That's an opportunity to put your refactoring chops to the test. How elegant can this system be? How much faster can you fix or enhance this section next time because of the refactoring you're doing this time?

As long as you're keeping it running and responding to user requests in a timely fashion, maintenance mode is a place of freedom and creativity. You are project leader, architect, designer, coder, and tester. You can flex your creative abilities all you like, and measurable success or failure of the system is yours to bear.

When you're maintaining a system, you can also plan for more visible improvements. Your three-year-old web system might not take advantage of some of the snappy new user interface features available to modern web browsers. If you can work it in between keeping the system running and making bug fixes, you could visibly enhance the user experience with the system. Adding a few well-placed bells and whistles your customers weren't expecting is not too different from surprising your wife with flowers or, as a kid, cleaning the house while your parents were out shopping. And, without the bureaucracy of a full-blown project underway, you'll be surprised at just how much you can fit into those cracks. Your customers will be too.

A hidden advantage of doing maintenance work is that, unlike the contractual environment of many of today's project teams, the maintenance programmer often has the opportunity to interact directly with his or her customers. This means that more people will know who you are, and you'll have the chance to build a larger base of advocates in your business. It also puts you in a prime spot for truly learning the inner workings of your business. If you're responsible for a business application in its entirety, always working with its end users through problems and questions, chances are that even without much effort, you will come to understand what the application actually does as well as many of its business users. Business rules are encoded into application logic that businesspeople can't usually read. I've seen many situations where it was only the maintenance programmers who fully understood how a specific business

---

12. For more on *broken windows*, see *The Pragmatic Programmer: From Journeyman to Master* [HT00].

process in a company worked. No one else had direct exposure to the authoritative encoding of that business logic.

The big irony surrounding the project vs. maintenance split is that project work *is* maintenance. As soon as your project team has written its first line of code, each additional feature is being grafted onto a living code base. Sure, the code might be cleaner or there might be less of it than if you were working on a legacy application, but the basic act is the same. New features are being added to and bugs are being fixed in existing code. Who knows how to do this better and faster than someone who has truly embraced maintenance programming and made it a mission to learn how to do it well?

Act on It!

1. *Measure, improve, measure*—For the most critical application or code that you maintain, make a list of *measurable* factors that represent the quality of the application. This might be response time for the application, number of unhandled exceptions that get thrown during processing, or application uptime. Or, if you handle support directly, don't directly assess quality for the *application*. Support request turnaround time (how fast you respond to and solve problems) is an important part of your users' experience with the application.

    Pick the most important of these measurable attributes, and start measuring it. After you have a good baseline measurement, set a realistic goal, and improve the application's (or your own) performance to meet that goal. After you've made an improvement, measure again to verify that you really made the improvement you wanted. If you have, share it with your team and your customers.

    Pick another metric, and do it again. After the first one, you'll find that it becomes fun, like a game. Measurably improving things like this gets addictive.

Eight-Hour Burn

One of the many sources of controversy around the Extreme Programming movement is its initial assertion that team members should work no more than forty hours per week. This kind of talk really upsets slave-driving managers who want to squeeze as much productivity as possible from their teams. It even kind of upset programmers themselves. The number of hours worked continuously becomes part of the developer machismo, like how many beers a frat boy can chug at a kegger.

Bob Martin,[13] one of the Extreme Programming community's luminaries, turned the phrase around in a way that made it much more tolerable for both parties while staying true to Kent Beck's original intent. Martin renamed *forty-hour workweek* to "eight-hour burn." The idea is that you should work so relentlessly that there is no way that you could continue longer than eight hours.

Before we go too deeply into the burn, why the emphasis on keeping the number of hours down anyway? This chapter is about getting things done. Shouldn't we be talking about working *more* hours?

When it comes to work, less really can be more. The primary reason cited by the Extreme Programmers is that when we're tired, we can't think as effectively as when we're rested. When we're burned out, we aren't as creative, and the quality of our work reduces dramatically. We start making stupid mistakes that end up costing us time and money.

Most projects last a long time. You can't keep up the pace of a sprint and finish a marathon. Though your short-term productivity will

> Projects are marathons, not sprints.

significantly increase as you start putting in the hours, in the long term you're going to crash so hard that the recovery time will be larger than the productivity gains you enjoyed during your eighty-hour weeks.

---

13. http://www.objectmentor.com

You can also think of your time in the same way you think of your money. When I was a teenager, working part-time jobs for minimum wage, I would have been happy to live off the amount of money that I *waste* now. I have so much more money available to me now than I did when I was a teenager that I tend to be less aware as I spend each dollar. Somehow, I was able to survive back then. I had a place to live, a car to drive, and food to eat.

I have the same things today. And, I don't lead a particularly extravagant lifestyle now. Apparently, when money was scarce, I found ways to be more efficient with my cash. And, the end result was essentially the same.

We treat scarce resources as being more valuable, and we make more efficient use of them. In addition to money matters, we can also apply this to our time. Think about day 4 of the last seventy-hour week you worked. No doubt, you were putting in a valiant effort. But, by day 4, you start to get lax with your time. *It's 10:30 a.m., and I know I'm going to be here for hours after everyone else goes home. I think I'll check out the latest technology news for a while.*

When you have too much time to work, your work time reduces significantly in perceived value. If you have seventy hours available, each hour is less precious to you than when you have forty hours available.

When the value of the dollar suffers from inflation, you need more dollars to buy the same stuff. When the value of the *hour* is deflated, you need more hours to *do* stuff. Bob Martin's eight-hour burn places a constraint on you and gives you a strategy for dealing with that constraint. You get to work and think, *I've only got eight hours! Go, go, go!* With strict barriers on start and end times, you naturally start to organize your time more effectively. You might start with a set of tasks that need to get done for the day, and you lay them out in prioritized order and start nailing them one at a time.

The eight-hour burn creates an environment that feels like that ultraproductive weekend you might have occasionally spent in college, cramming for a test in a course that you had been neglecting or jamming out a term paper that had fallen prey to procrastination. The difference is that this is constrained *cramming*. Times of cramming are usually extremely productive, because time becomes scarce and therefore extremely valuable. The eight-hour burn is a method of cramming early and often without having to stay up all night taking NoDoze and drinking Jolt Cola.

As thought workers, even if we're not in front of a computer or in the office, we can be working. You might be working while you're driving to dinner with your spouse or while you're watching a movie. Your work is following you around nagging you.

My work usually nags me when I haven't paid enough attention to it. I might be letting a specific task slip or letting tasks pile up and not taking care of them. This is when the work follows me home and badgers me while I'm trying to relax. If you work intensely every day, you'll find that the work doesn't follow you home. Not only are you deliberately stopping yourself from working after-hours, but your mind will actually *allow* you to stop working after-hours.

Budget your work hours carefully. Work less, and you'll accomplish more. Work is always more welcome when you've given yourself time away from it.

Act on It!

1. Make sure you sleep well tonight. Tomorrow, eat breakfast and then start work at an exact time (preferably a little earlier than usual). Work intensely for four hours. Take an hour lunch. Then work for four more hours so intensely that you are absolutely exhausted and can't do any more. Go home, relax, and have fun.

Learn How to Fail

As programmers, we know that the sooner in the development process that we can discover software failures, the more robust the software is going to be. Unit testing helps us ferret out the strange bugs as early as we can. If we discover bizarre errors in our own code, if they happen early, we are happy. Though they signify a small failure on our part as developers—we made a programming error—finding them early and often is a good sign of what the health of the software will become.

We are taught to allow our programming errors to be loud and messy early on. You want to know about them when they happen so you can put the correct fixes or defensive measures in place. When you're coding, you don't go out of your way to silence the little software failures that are destined to arise during development. That is the code's way of talking to you. Those little failures are part of the strengthening process. So, we add assertions that crash our programs when something goes wrong or unit tests that turn a bar red if we goof up.

The little failures we encounter also teach us what kind of failures to expect. If you've never walked through a minefield before, you might not know which lumps of dirt *not* to step on. If your software hasn't been complaining to you regularly, you might not know where the dangerous nooks and crannies are. You can program just so defensively when you're coding blind.

Furthermore, it's important to program defensively. Software quality is really put to the test when things go wrong. It's inevitable that *something* will happen for which you did not build a contingency case. Segfaults and blue screens in production code mean that the programmers didn't do a good job of dealing with the failures they couldn't foresee.

The same principles apply on the job. A craftsperson is really put to the test when the errors arise. Learning to deal with mistakes is a skill that is both highly valuable

> Every wrong note is but one step away from a right one.

and difficult to teach. As a jazz improviser, I learned that every wrong note is at most one step away from a right one. What makes improvisations bad is when the improviser doesn't know what to do when the wrong note pops out. Standing in front of a band on one side and an audience on another, the sound of a real stinker of a note is enough to freeze an amateur to the bone. Even the masters play wrong notes. But they recover in such a way that the listener can't tell that the whole thing wasn't intentional.

We're all going to make stupid mistakes on the job. It's part of being human. We make coding mistakes that lead to customers looking at stack traces. We paint ourselves into corners with critical design mistakes. Or, worse, we say the wrong things to our team members, managers, and customers. We make bad commitments or false claims about what we're capable of doing. Or we accidentally give our team members bad advice on how to solve a technical problem, wasting hours of their time.

Because we all make mistakes, we also know that everyone else makes mistakes. So, within reason, we don't judge each other on the mistakes we make. We judge each other on how we deal with those inevitable mistakes.

Whether it is a technical, communication, or project management mistake, the following rules apply:

- Raise the issue as early as you know about it. Don't try to hide it for any length of time. As in software development and testing, mistakes caught early are less of a problem than mistakes caught late. The earlier you suck it up and expose what you've done, the less the negative impact is likely to have.

- Take the blame. Don't try to look for a scapegoat even if you can find a good one. Even if you're not wholly to blame, take responsibility and move on. The goal is to move past this point as quickly as possible. A problem needs a resolution. Lingering on whose fault it is only prolongs the issue.

- Offer a solution. If you don't have one, offer a plan of attack for finding a solution. Speak in terms of concrete, predictable time frames. If you've designed your team into a corner, give time frames on when you will get back with an assessment of the effort required to reverse the issue. Concrete, attainable goals, even if small and immaterial, are important at this stage. Not only do they keep things moving from bad to good, but they help to rebuild credibility in the process.

- Ask for help. Even if you are solely to blame for a problem, don't let your pride make it worse by refusing help in a resolution. Your team members, management, and customers will look at you in a much more positive light if you can maintain a healthy attitude and set your ego aside while the team helps you dig your way out. Too often, we feel a sense of responsibility that drives us to proudly shoulder a burden too large, and we end up thrashing unproductively until someone forcibly intervenes.

Think about the last time you experienced a customer service issue at a restaurant. Perhaps you waited way too long for the *wrong dish* to ultimately reach your table. Think about how the waiter reacted to your complaint.

> Stressful times offer the best opportunities to build loyalty.

The wrong reaction is for the waiter to make excuses or to blame the cooks. The wrong reaction would be for the waiter to walk off to resubmit the order and stay out of sight while you sit there starving and wondering when the hell your food is finally going to arrive. Of the course, the *really* wrong reaction would be for the waiter to arrive with a dish that he already knows is wrong, hoping you would either not notice or not complain.

The difference between how a company treats us when they make a mistake can be the ultimate in loyalty building (or destroying). A mistake handled well might make us more loyal customers than we would have been had we never experienced a service problem. Remember this with *your* customers whenever you make mistakes on the job.

Say "No"

The quickest path to missing your commitments is to make commitments that you know you can't meet. I know that sounds patently obvious, but we do it every day. We are put on the spot and we don't want to disappoint our leaders, so we agree to impossible work being done in impossible timelines.

Saying "yes" is an addictive and destructive habit. It's a bad habit masquerading as a good one. But there's a big difference between a *can-do* attitude and the misrepresentation of one's capabilities. The latter causes problems not only for you but for the people to whom you are making your promises. If I am your manager and I ask you whether you can rewrite the way we track shipments in our company's fulfillment system by the end of the month, chances are that I asked specifically about the end of the month for a reason. Someone probably asked *me* if it could be done by then. Or there might be another critical business change we're trying to make that is dependent on the fulfillment system. So, armed with your assurance that you can make the date, I run off and commit to my customers that it will be done.

> Saying "yes" to avoid disappointment is just lying.

Saying "yes" in this way is as good as lying. I'm not saying it's malicious. We lie to ourselves as much as we do to those we make the commitments to. After all, saying "no" feels bad. We are programmed to want to always succeed. And, saying we *can't* do something feels like we failed.

What we humans fail to internalize is that "yes" is not always the right answer. And, "no" is seldom the wrong answer. I say internalize, because I think we all *know* this to be true. After all, none of us wants to be the recipient of false commitments.

The inability to say "no" happens to be a common part of the Indian culture. Companies that are inexperienced with offshore outsourcing almost always run into it. You learn with time to sniff out uncertainty and ask the right questions. Enough "one more day until it's done" conversations naturally train you to probe deeper. And, it's not only a part of the IT culture. When I lived in Bangalore, I stayed home from work no less than five times waiting for a cable modem installation that never happened. It turned out that for the first three times the company didn't even have the parts required to do the installation when they made the appointment. But, they didn't want to disappoint me. I told them I was hoping to have the cable modem installed next week, so they promised that it would be installed, knowing full well that the installation was not going to be possible next week.

Though the intent is positive, the ramifications are negative. I eventually got a little nasty with my cable modem installers and even made them come to my house on a holiday to do the installation. I didn't trust the promise that it would be installed "tomorrow, after the holiday." Repeatedly missing commitments had destroyed any chance I had of trusting them. In fact, I had developed a sense of hostility toward them.

On the other hand, what happens when you're asked to do a critical task and you say that you can't? As a manager of both onshore and offshore teams, I can tell you that "no" has become a source of relief to me. If I have a team member who has the strength to say "no" when that's the truth, then I know that when they say "yes," they really mean it. A commitment from someone like this is going to be more credible and carry a lot of weight. If they actually hit the targets that they commit to, I'm not going to question them when they say they *can't* hit one.

If someone always says "yes," they're either incredibly talented or lying. The latter is usually the case.

"I don't know" is also a great thing to say when it's appropriate. You might be responding to whether you can meet a date and need time to research the task before committing. Or you might be asked how a technology works or how some piece of your project's code is implemented. Just as in the case of commitments, not knowing the answer to something feels like a small failure. But, your co-workers and managers will have more faith in you when you claim to know something. You'll notice that when you meet a real guru in a subject area, they're never afraid to admit when they don't know something. "I don't know" is not a phrase for the insecure.

That same courage can also come in handy when dealing with decisions from above. How many times have you seen a technology decision dictated by a manager who caused the team members to sit around the table quietly looking at their shoes and waiting for the chance to escape the meeting room so they could complain to each other? Managers are often the target of the *Emperor's New Clothes* phenomenon. Everyone knows that a decision is bad, but they're all afraid to speak up. As a manager, I make decisions or strong suggestions all the time. However, I don't hire my employees to be robots. It's the ones who speak up and offer a better suggestion that become my trusted lieutenants.

Don't go overboard with the "no" game. Can-do attitudes are still appreciated, and it's good to have stretch goals. If you're not sure you can do something, but you want to give it a try, say that. "This is going to be a challenge, but I'd like to give it a try" is a wonderful answer. Sometimes, of course, the answer is simply "yes."

Be courageous enough to be honest.

Act on It!

1. Karl Brophey, a reviewer, suggests keeping a list of every commitment you make:

    -   What was asked of you for a due date?

    -   What did you commit to?

    -   If you were overridden, record both what you thought and what you were told to accept.

    -   Record when you delivered.

    Examine this daily. Communicate where you'll fail as soon as you know. Examine this monthly—what is your hit rate? How often are you right on?

Don't Panic

I started my career as a computer programmer because of video games. Since the days of loading games from tape on my Commodore 64, I've been hooked by their immersive, interactive experiences. I used to be embarrassed to admit it, but I realize now that it's nothing to be ashamed of. For me, computer games turned the on-screen environment (the operating system, I guess) into an environment I was comfortable and excited about.

My favorite game ever was id Software's Doom. I was specifically in love with the one-on-one, player-vs.-player, death-match part of the game. Players would connect via modem or serial connection and battle each other in small, fast-paced environments. I got really good at the Doom death match. I often joke that it might be the thing in my life so far that I'm best at. The game of death match is surprisingly complex. It's both technical and psychological—like a frenetic mix of chess and fencing on fast-forward.

Like most skills, a great way to get good at it is to watch masters at work. Back in my Doom days, there was one such master who went by the ironic online handle "Noskill." Noskill was the de facto reigning Doom champion. People from around North America would pay the long-distance telephone fees to try their luck against him. These matches would all be recorded with Doom's built-in game-recording facility. I watched every one.

It didn't take me long to learn his secret. Sure, he was generally good at the game, but there was one obvious key to his success: he never panicked. Doom was the kind of game in which a round could be over literally seconds after it started. It was really fast. I remember my first death-match game. Spawn, die, spawn, die, spawn, die. When I finally managed to stay alive more than a couple of seconds I found myself running around aimlessly, barely able to keep track of where I was.

But Noskill never acted that way. No matter how difficult the situation, you could tell by watching the recordings that he was always relaxed and always thinking about what to do next. He was always seemingly aware of how his current context fit into the overall shape of the match.

Now if you think about other games, particularly sports, you'll recognize that the best players all

Heroes never panic.

share this quality. In fact, even the characters we admire in books, television, and movies share this quality. Heroes never panic. They're always the people who can have a nuclear bomb dropped on their city or crash in an airplane and manage to organize a group, help the survivors, outsmart the enemy, or at least just not break down in tears.

This extends to real life, too. Despite my best planning, my professional life has been a string of emergencies and disasters. Projects run really really late. Software applications crash, costing my employers money and credibility. I say the wrong thing to the wrong vice president and gain a political enemy. Most of the time, these things come in waves all together, never one at a time.

In my worst moments, I panic. I lock up and can think tactically at best. I react to each small input without the clarity to consider the big picture.

But looking back on literally *every* such disaster, not a single one has made a lasting, noticeable impact on me or my career. So, as panicked or depressed or upset as I've gotten over these seemingly disastrous situations, not one has been a *true* disaster.

What did the panicking give me? What was the advantage of reacting negatively to each of these situations? Nothing. What panicking really gave me was an inability to perform at my best at the times I really *needed* to be performing at my best.

Now I have to admit that not panicking in stressful situations is easier said than done. It's kind of like telling someone "just be happy." Sure, it's good advice, but how do you do it? How do you avoid panicking when things seem to be falling apart? To answer this question, it helps to think a little about why we *do* panic.

We panic because we lose perspective. When something is going wrong, it's hard not to focus all attention on the problem. To some extent, that's a good way to solve problems. Unfortunately, it also makes the problem, no matter how small, seem more important than it is. And with the problem inflated and stress levels running high, our brains turn themselves off.

Who is the worst computer user you know? For me, it's probably one of my parents or in-laws (I know who, but I'm smart enough not to name any names here). Imagine that person sitting at their computer trying to finish a project when an error message start popping up with everything they try to do. We've all seen this happen. Inexperienced computer users get quickly frustrated and freaked out. They start hectically clicking and dragging things around on the screen, ignoring the potentially helpful error message text as it pops up over and over again. They eventually get so flustered that they have to call for help, but usually not before messing up one or two additional things on the computer before doing so.

Don't think I'm mean, but I want you to picture this situation with someone appropriate you know as the main character, and I want you to laugh to yourself about it. This kind of behavior really is ridiculous, isn't it? It's laughable.

But, as genuinely funny as this is, what we just imagined was a real-life scenario in which a person working outside their comfort zone encountered a problem and panicked. It's no different from the way I've reacted when projects have run late or I've accidentally crashed a system or I've dissatisfied a customer on the job. It's just a different context.

So, here's how I'm learning to not panic. When something bad happens and I start to feel that sinking, stressed-out feeling that leads to panic, I compare myself to the frustrated computer-illiterate, and I laugh at myself. I analyze the situation from the third-person perspective, as if I'm helping that frustrated family member with their word processing disaster. Seemingly hard problems are suddenly easier. Seemingly bad situations are suddenly not so bad. And, I often find that the solution simple and staring me in the face in the same way that an error dialog often tells you exactly what to do next. If you'd just have the presence of mind to read the error message, the problem might be solved.

Act on It!

1. Keep a panic journal. The key to catching panic before it happens is to develop a heightened real-time awareness of your perception and emotions as they happen. I've had my best luck learning to do this

by analyzing my reactions to situations after the fact. I'm not smart enough to naturally keep a background thread running and analyzing my thoughts as they happen, but I've discovered that if I practice the analysis "offline," I get better and better at doing the analysis in real time.

Saying you're going to do a better job of analyzing your reactions and actually doing it are two different things. Keeping a journal will help add structure to the process. Each day at a specific time (use a calendar with a reminder!), open up a text file and record any situation that caused you to panic, even if only a little bit. Once a week, look back on the past week's list and take stock of the lasting impact of each panic-inducing situation. Was the situation panic-worthy? What would have been the most productive reaction to the situation? What would the hero in a dramatized movie about your life have done instead of panicking?

After some practice, you'll find the analysis to start happening *while* the panic sets in. As you rationally explore the reasons for your panic in real time, you'll find that the panic itself takes a backseat and eventually dissipates.

Say It, Do It, Show It

The easiest way to never get anything done is to never commit to anything. If you don't have a deadline, you don't have any pressure or much incentive to finish something. This is especially true when the *something* that needs to get done isn't 100 percent exciting.

Even a bad manager's instinct usually tells them that it's important to plan. For some developers, the invocation of the word *plan* is cause for alarm. Endless meetings with pointy-haired bosses creating reams of printed Microsoft Project plans that nobody understands or uses are a valid cause for alarm. So, techies often overcompensate in our rebellion against perceived overplanning by constantly flying by the seat of our pants.

Planning isn't such bad-tasting medicine that we should have to hold our breath to force it down. Planning can be a liberating experience. When you have too much to do, a plan can make the difference between confused ambiguity at the start of a workday and clear-headed confidence when attacking the tasks ahead.

Plans don't have to be big and drawn out. A list in a text document or e-mail is perfectly fine. Plans don't have to cover a large span of time. Being able to start the day and answer the question "What are you going to do today?" is a great first step. I know many people whose days stay so hectic that they would almost always fail this test. A good first step would be to find time this afternoon and list everything you want to get done on the next workday and arrange them in priority order. Try to be realistic about what can fill a day, though you're likely to be wrong and specifically likely to overcommit yourself.

You can be as detailed or as loose as you want with your one-day plan. I had a roommate in college named Chris who would wake up every morning and, even at risk of being late for his first class, would meticulously plan out his day, specifically focusing on his piano practice schedule (he was a jazz piano major). His schedule was fairly rigid already with the selection of classes he had to attend. Still,

Chris would actually plan down to how he was going to use the fifteen minutes *between* classes to fit in practice routines that could be done quickly. Many of his classes were in the same building, so it was common to have plenty of leisure time in between them for some quick socializing or grabbing a drink from the vending machines. Chris would be cramming in scales or ear training while the rest of us were sitting around waiting for the next class to start. He would even divide his schedule into multiple three-to-five-minute segments, so he could fit more than one practice exercise into a given ten-minute period. Chris ended up becoming one of the most respected musicians in our city. Natural talent had something to do with it, of course, but I've since held the belief that he planned and executed his way into the musical elite.

So, you've made your plan. It may not be as detailed as Chris's, but it's enough to answer the question of what you're going to do with your day. When you get to work tomorrow, pull out the list and start on the first item. Work through the list until you go to lunch, and then pick up where you left off and try to finish the list.

As you complete each item on the list, mark it DONE. Use capital letters. Say the word, *done*. Be happy. At the end of the day, look at your list of DONE stuff and feel like you've accomplished something. Not only did you know what you were going to do today, but now you know what you've *done*.

If you didn't get everything done, don't worry about it. You knew you weren't going to be right about how much would fit in a day anyway. Just move the incomplete items from today (if they're still relevant) onto tomorrow's list, and start the process again. It's a stimulating process. It's rhythmic. It allows you to divide your days and weeks into a series of small victories, each one propelling you to the next. You'll find that not only does it give you visibility into what you're accomplishing, but you'll actually get *more done* than if you weren't watching things so closely.

Having established a rhythm of plan and attack, you are ready to start thinking in terms of weeks and even months. Of course, the larger the time span you're planning for, the higher level your plan should get. Think of week and day plans as being tactical battle plans, with thirty-, sixty-, and ninety-day plans focusing on more strategic goals that you want to accomplish.

The very act of thinking about what you want to have accomplished in ninety days is something unnatural for software soldiers on the field. We are tactical people. Forcing yourself to imagine an end state for your system, your team's processes, or your career after ninety days will cause things to surface that you never expected. The view from above the field shows us very different things than the view from the ground. It will be difficult at first, but stick with it. Like all good skills, it gets easier with practice, and the benefits will be visible to both you and those who work with you (even if they don't know that you are doing it).

Status reports can help you market yourself. You should start communicating your plans to your management. The best time to start communicating the plans is after you have executed at least one cycle of the plan. And—this is an important point—start doing it before they ask you to do it. No manager in his or her right mind would be unhappy to receive a *succinct* weekly e-mail from an employee stating what was accomplished in the past week and what they plan to do in the next. Receiving this kind of regular message unsolicited is a manager's dream.

Start by communicating week by week. When you've gotten comfortable with this process, start working in your thirty-, sixty-, and ninety-day plans. On the longer views, stick to high-level, impactful progress you plan to make on projects or systems you maintain. Always state these long-term plans as proposals to your manager, and ask for feedback. Over time, these anticipation attempts will require less tweaking from your managers as you learn which items usually go unedited and which are the subject of more thrashing.

The most critical factor to keep in mind with everything that goes onto a plan is that it should always be accounted for later. Every item must be either visibly completed, delayed, removed, or replaced. No items should go unaccounted for. If items show up on a plan and are never mentioned again, people will stop trusting your plans, and the plans and you will counteract the effectiveness of planning. Even if the outcome is *bad*, you should communicate it as such. We all make mistakes. The way to differentiate yourself is to address your mistakes or inabilities publicly and ask for help resolving them. Consistently tracing tasks on a plan will create the deserved impression that no important work is getting lost in the mix.

Get this process going, and suddenly in the eyes of your management you have exposed your strategic side. Creating and executing plans shows that you are not just a robot typing code, but you are a *leader*. It's this kind of independent productivity that companies need as they reduce overhead.

A final benefit of communicating in terms of plans is that your commitments become more credible. If you say what you're going to do and then you do it and show that it's done, you develop a reputation for being a *doer*. With credibility comes influence. Imagine you want to introduce a new process, such as an agile development practice,[14] into an organization or you want to bring in a new technology. With the proven ability to make and meet commitments, you'll be granted more leeway to try new things.

In our Bangalore software center, we had a team that had been working night shifts for more than a year. Of the seven members on the team, two were always on the night shift. They rotated weekly, so every third or fourth week, each team member would switch to a 7 p.m. to 3 a.m. schedule. The team was getting frustrated and burnt out, saying that they almost constantly felt jet-lagged. But, the team was playing a critical support role, and the team's U.S.-based internal customers were convinced they couldn't get by without live real-time help from the group in Bangalore.

So, the team put together a plan of attack. They looked at their various support processes and associated measurements and crafted a plan to both switch back to a single-day shift *and* to make significant improvements in their customer experience, simultaneously. As acting operations leader of the software center, I helped them fine-tune their plan and was present (as moral support) for the formal proposal they made to their manager in the United States.

They knew this was going to be a touchy subject for their manager, who had to answer to his U.S.-based customers in person. There was naturally much trepidation among the team members as the meeting started. However, the team's manager was so impressed that he immediately and happily signed off on the proposal, and the team put its plan into action. Within weeks, the jet lag was over, and everyone was back on day shifts.

---

14. http://www.agilemanifesto.org

The solidity of their plan for how to not only deal with the change in work hours but how they were going to strategically improve the performance of their team inspired great confidence in the leaders and, eventually, their customers. The team's manager used the plan when communicating the change with his customers. And, the team followed through. Within months, the team was running at a new level of efficiency. They've since gained such credibility and confidence that they have taken more and more ownership and independence over the workings of their team.

The team used its plan as a concrete response to a problem. They came to their manager not with complaints but with proposed solutions.

Your leaders want you to have independence and ownership. Making, executing, and communicating plans will help you attain both.

Failing and Copying

by Patrick Collison

Larry Wall wrote that the traits of a great programmer are laziness, impatience, and hubris. I don't know whether these are innate or whether they can be acquired with diligent self-improvement. Either way, it's not obvious how one can use this information to become a better programmer. So, instead of looking at traits, we should look at activities that will help in improvement.

If I had to pick two, I'd pick failing and copying.

I fail more than most programmers I know. Certainly, a majority of my projects fail. Sitting in ~/Projects are a bunch of neglected efforts to do something interesting, each about as likely to break out and succeed as a lobster is to swim free from its pot. They're kinda interesting. Like families, successful projects are alike, but every unsuccessful project fails in its own way.

And although it's almost a cliché to say that having a failed company behind you is great experience, I haven't heard the same idea extended to programming much.

(I'm good at both, though. I've had failed businesses too.)

Commercial failure tends to build a very direct kind of experience. You learn the importance of conserving cash, or you become more determined. But with programming, it's not so much the experience of failing that's valuable as the knowledge gained in working on the kind of projects that are likely to fail.

When I started programming, a lot my time was spent failing to write all kinds of fascinating things: operating systems, file systems, virtual machines, reimplementations of network protocols, interpreters, and JIT compilers. Most of them never worked properly, and those that did were still pretty bad. Of course, even ignoring the technical aspects, most were doomed from the start. I'm not sure what fraction of 1 percent the success rate for new operating systems is, but it's small.

Failing and Copying (continued)

Still, for me, these projects are programming at its most enjoyable. They're the fundamental problems of software engineering stripped of anything extraneous. They're all about trade-offs in space, speed, reliability, and complexity, without a rounded corner or buggy API in sight.

They're the kind of pure problems that you can become absorbed in for months and still not emerge with something that works—as I regularly demonstrated.

I'm not sure exactly why, but people learning to program today don't seem to experience this as much.

I think it may be at least partially because the rise of web-based software. Just a few days ago, someone on Hacker News asked whether there's anyone still interested in writing client-side software. It's an exaggeration, but it's not too far from the truth. And hey, web-based software really is very cool.

From a programming standpoint, though, this shift has a drawback. Web apps rarely involve tough technical challenges until the scale becomes huge (Internet Explorer 6 compatibility notwithstanding).

In other words, the barrier to entry for failure is higher. You have to become successful first.

So, especially given this movement towards web-based software, I think it's important to actively seek out failure-prone projects.

What about copying? To become a better programmer, anyone will tell you that you should read good code. Even though they presumably don't mean it literally (that's far too boring), "reading" remains, at heart, the wrong idea: it's passive. Instead, I think you have to actively copy, widely and unashamedly.

This applies to a lot of things, of course. Hunter S. Thompson didn't just read good books; he typed out Hemingway and Fitzgerald. And the oldest known Bach manuscripts are transcriptions Bach made of works by other organists. More famously, maybe, Gates fished programs out of trash cans at Harvard.

Failing and Copying (continued)

It's not too hard to see how this helps. Copying builds muscle memory. You get a feel for the nuance and form of the original—the kind of detail that's lost in a quick scan.

In the case of code, there's also a less obvious—but significant—benefit. Copying lets you go further with projects that are likely to fail. This can be straightforward transcription of, say, a hash-table implementation (which made the first interpreter I wrote suck a lot less) or a design that's just inspired and shaped by the original (as, say, Linux was by Minix).

At its best, this leads to a sort of virtuous cycle of failing and copying, where it becomes a kind of lazily evaluated self-improvement. You tackle something hard, stumble up against some insurmountable problem, copy someone else's solution, and, hey, you now know how to do whatever it was.

In this unrestrained looting, as you wholeheartedly absorb various techniques, you often figure out how to put them together in some new way. I'm not sure what Picasso meant by "Good artists copy, while great artists steal." Maybe he was just being intentionally perverse, but the former meaning is what I've always assumed.

Programming is full of odd ideas. Using shorter, less descriptive names often produces code that's more readable overall. The most powerful languages usually have far fewer concepts than the lesser ones. And failing and copying may be the best way to produce successful, original work.

Patrick Collison is a student at MIT.

Part IV

Marketing… Not Just for Suits

You are the most talented software developer you know. Elegant designs flow out of the seemingly unending river of your creativity. Your architectural insightfulness is unmatched in your workplace. You can code faster and more accurately than anyone your company has ever employed.

So what?

Many software developers—especially the most conceited ones, it seems—live with the misconception that their skill should be self-evident to any clued-in manager or employer. They are able to comfortably veil this lie inside the cloud of a make-believe moral ethic: they're just too *humble* to market their own abilities. Going out of their way to make their abilities known would be *brownnosing*. No self-respecting programmer would be caught dead sucking up to The Man.

This is all just an excuse. Actually, they're afraid.

Most programmer types were the last kids picked for every team when they were in school. They probably avoided social situations where possible and failed miserably where not possible. It's no surprise that these people are afraid to stick their necks out by trying to show someone their capabilities.

Suspending disbelief for a minute, let's pretend the moral ethic nonsense isn't such a put-on after all. Regardless of one's intentions, it's stupid not to let people know what you're capable of doing. Think of it this way: you are employed to develop software that adds value to a company. The job of a leader is to develop teams that deliver the maximum amount of value to the company. How is a leader to do his or her job without knowing who in an organization is capable of what kind of work?

As one manager told me recently, if someone does something truly fantastic and nobody knows about it, in his eyes it didn't happen. It may sound ruthless, but from a company's perspective it makes sense. Pragmatically speaking, managers don't have time to keep close tabs on what each employee is doing every day. And neither companies nor their employees would want managers spending their time this way. Companies want managers focusing on the big picture—not tracking daily tasks. And employees (especially programmers) hate to be micromanaged.

In short, you may have the best product in history, but if you don't do some kind of advertising, nobody is going to buy it. We all know—especially in the software world—that the best product doesn't always win. There's a lot more to success in the marketplace than having a great product. Let's not forget this truth in the job market.

Enough already…what should I do?

On the surface, marketing yourself is simple. You have only two goals: to let people know you exist and to let them know you are the person who can solve the tough problems that keep them up at night. This applies not only to the job market at large but also to the company at which you currently work. Don't assume that just because you're employed with a company, its management knows who you are. Furthermore, don't assume that just because a leader knows your name that he or she has even the faintest understanding of your capabilities.

This part will not only help make sure your current leaders understand what you're capable of, but it will show you how to expand your scope to the industry at large. In the book so far, we've talked about how to be marketable. Now we're going to learn how to put that marketability into action.

Perceptions, Perschmeptions

It's comfortable to play the idealist and pretend you don't care what other people think about you. But, that's a game. You can't let yourself believe it. You *should* care what other people think about you. Perception is reality. Get over it.

You probably know the old clichéd philosophical question, "If a tree falls in the forest but nobody is there to hear it fall, did it make a sound?" The correct answer to the question is, "Who cares?"

I mean, the fall probably made a sound. That's not a very exciting answer on a metaphysical level, but it probably did. But, if nobody heard it fall, then the fact that it made a sound doesn't really matter.

The same goes for your work. If you kick ass and no one is there to see, did you really kick ass? Who cares? No one.

In the subculture of Indian IT bureaucracy, I was amazed at how people just didn't *get* this simple truth. Almost everyone I dealt with there didn't understand why it should matter that their managers, for example, knew what they were doing. If *you* knew you were better than so and so, then it should be reflected in your performance reviews, ratings, and salary. They had fooled themselves into thinking that how other people perceived them was somehow subservient to the *truth*, whatever that was.

This truth thing…what is it? Who defines it? What is good and what is bad in an absolute sense?

The answer is that there is no absolute good or bad, at least not in terms of judging who is better at a creative, knowledge worker job. How do you define what makes a good song? What about a good painting? You might have your own definitions, but I doubt I would agree with them. They're subjective.

Performance appraisals are never objective.

Horrible risk-averse human resources departments in horrible risk-averse companies spin their wheels chasing objective measures of the people they employ. Sometimes they even implement "objective" appraisal systems. All of my team members in India thought *they* wanted to be measured this way. That's because they had never experienced it before.

There is no way to objectively measure the quality of a knowledge worker, and there is no way to objectively measure the quality of their work. Go ahead. Disagree. Now think about your argument for a while. See the holes?

So, if the measure of your goodness at your company (or in the industry or the job market or wherever) is subjective, what does that mean? That means you are always going to be measured based on someone else's *perception* of you. Your potential promotions or salary increases—even the decision of whether you should continue to be on the payroll at all—is completely dependent on the perceptions of others.

Subjectivity, being based on *personal* taste, implies that you can't count on any two opinions being the same. Different people are impressed with different factors. Some people might like rigid structure, while others prefer loose, free creativity. Some may prefer to communicate via e-mail and others face to face or by phone. Some managers may like their employees to be aggressive, while others prefer them to act like subordinates. You say "Poh tay toh"—I say "poh tah toh."

It doesn't come down only to personal preference. People in different roles and relationships to you build their perceptions based on the qualities most important to making *that particular* relationship work well. If I'm a project manager, the quality of your source code is a lot less important to me than the quality of your communications. If I'm a fellow programmer, your raw ability and creativity drive my perception of you more than, for example, your follow-through. But, if I'm your manager, raw ability is ultimately meaningless to me unless you actually *do* something with it.

We've culturally trained ourselves to *perceive* that managing perception is somehow a dirty and shameful activity. But, as you can see, managing perception is just practical. When you explicitly take note of the factors that drive other people's perceptions of you, you more firmly discover how to make them happy customers. You're not going to impress your nontechnical business client with your object-oriented design skills. You might be a design genius, but if you can't communicate effectively and you don't manage to complete your work on time, your customers will think you stink. It's not their fault. You *do* stink.

Perceptions really do matter. They keep you employed (or unemployed). They get you promoted or get you stuck in the same job for years. They give you raises or lowball you on salary. The sooner you get over yourself and learn to manage perceptions, the sooner you'll be on the right track.

Act on It!

1. Perceptions are driven by different factors, depending on who the audience is. Your mother doesn't much care how well you can design object-oriented systems, but your teammates might.

   Understanding what's important in each of your relationships is an important part of building credible perceptions with those you interact with. Think about the different classes of relationships you generally have with people in the office. For example, you probably have teammates who do the same type of job you do. You also probably have a direct manager, and you may have one or more customers and a project manager.

   Take these different groups (or whichever actually apply given the structure of your workplace), and list them. Next to each, write down which of your attributes is most likely to drive that group's perception of you. Here's an example:

Group	Perception Drivers
Teammates	Technical skills, social skills, teamwork.
Manager	Leadership ability, customer focus, communication skills, follow through, teamwork.
Customers	Customer focus, communication skills, follow through.
Project manager	Communication skills, follow through, productivity, technical skills.

   Put some thought into your own list. How might you change your behavior as a result of this list? In what ways have you already been adjusting your focus as you interact with each group? In what ways have you *not* been appropriately adjusting your behavior?

Adventure Tour Guide

At the risk of stating the obvious, the most important aspect of getting the word out in the workplace is your ability to communicate. Gone are the days of the disheveled hacker crouching over his terminal and coding by the light of his monitor in the deepest bowels of the server room. The occasional monosyllabic grunt between feats of wizardry isn't gonna cut it.

As disturbing a proposition as it may be, put yourself into the mind of a manager or customer (I'll just use the word *customer* throughout this section to refer to both).

They're responsible for something gravely important that they ultimately have to entrust to some scary IT guys for implementation. They do what they can to help move things along, but ultimately they're at the mercy of these programmers. Moreover, they have no idea how to control them or even to communicate intelligently about what it is that they're doing. In this situation, what's the most important attribute they'll be looking for in a team member? I'll bet you the price of this book it's not whether they've memorized the latest design patterns or how many programming languages they know.

They're going to be looking for someone who can make them comfortable about the project they're working on.

These managers and customers we're talking about have a dirty little secret: they are *afraid* of you. And for good reason. You're

> Your customers are afraid of you.

smart. You speak a cryptic language they don't understand. You make them feel stupid with your sometimes sarcastic comments (which you might not have even intended to be sarcastic). And, your work is often the last and most important toll gate between a project's conception and its birth.

Your job is to be your customer's tour guide through the unforgiving terrain of the information technology world. You will make your customers comfortable while guiding them through an unfamiliar place. You will show them the sights and take them where they want to go while avoiding the seedy parts of town you've encountered in the past.

Nonprogrammers are, on the average, as intelligent as programmers. (That is to say that most of them aren't very intelligent, but a few of them really are.) Chances are high that your customer is just as smart as you but just doesn't happen to know how to program a computer. That's OK. You probably don't know how to do much of what he or she does on a daily basis. That's why there are two of you, and you're both being paid to come to work.

I mention the bit about intelligence because computer people all too often assume that anyone who doesn't know how to operate a computer is not intelligent. Saying it explicitly like this makes it sound idiotic, but that's true of all prejudices. However, this feeling is so ingrained in many of us that we don't even know when we're feeling it. Explicitly trying to control it doesn't work.

My advice is to reverse the relationship. Instead of feeling like you are the computer genius, descending from computer heaven to save your poor customer from purgatory, turn the tables around. If you're, for example, working in the insurance industry, think of your customer as a subject matter expert in insurance from which *you* have to learn in order to get *your* job done.

That being said, you need to be cognizant that your customers may need topics toned down a bit when you're discussing software-related matters. There's a delicate balance between too techie and too dumb.

"Why all this talk of how to treat your customers? I thought we were going to talk about how to market myself." If you work in a typical IT shop, much of the budget that keeps you gainfully employed comes from a business function—the same business function for which your customers work and influence decisions. When promotion and staffing decisions are being made, the best advocate you can have is a customer who doesn't want to live without you. On the flip side, imagine the impact of a customer who thinks you are condescending. Your customer represents the needs of the business, and you are paid to provide for those needs. Don't forget this.

Act on It!

1. *Check yourself*—Are you the grumpy old code ogre everyone fears? Are you *sure*? Are they afraid to tell you?

Go through your mailbox, and find examples of e-mails that you have sent to less-technical co-workers, managers, and customers. As you read through, try to see things from the recipient's perspective. If some time has passed since sending the messages, you'll be able to see yourself as a third-party observer would.

Even better, show the e-mails to your mom. Tell her that someone you work with sent the messages to a customer, and ask her how the messages would make *her* feel.

2. *Hop the fence*—Find an opportunity to be flung into a situation in which you are *not* the expert and are thus dependent on others who are.

    If you have two left feet, imagine yourself on a soccer team. If you have two left thumbs, imagine that you're part of the National Knitting Team. How would you like your teammates to communicate with you?

Me Rite Reel Nice

The days of the monosyllabic programmer grunt are over. If companies want to have difficulty communicating with their programmers, they'll sit the programmers on a different continent and in a different time zone and communicate with them only via e-mail and phone.

So, the communication issue is an important one. On the list of tasks you need to do to stay gainfully employed, it might sound a little contrived, silly, or trivial. You might feel a bit like you're back in high-school English class. That's OK. You can actually pay attention this time.

We'll get the most boring one over with first: grammar and spelling are important. You probably have a degree in an advanced subject like engineering or computer science, and here I am telling you to learn how to spell. *The nerve!*

But, at least here in the United States, we have a problem.

According to a report by the National Commission on Writing, more than half of all responding companies consider writing skills when making both hiring and promotion decisions. Forty percent of surveyed companies in the services sector said that a third or fewer of their new hires had the writing skills they desired.[15]

When you really step back and take a look at the big picture, writing skills are both necessary *and* are in short supply.

As you know, the world's workforce is distributing itself globally. As this trend continues, there will come a time—for some, that time is now!—when *most* workplace communication will take place in written form via either instant messaging or e-mail.

You're going to be writing *a lot*. If so much of your job is going to involve writing, you better get good at it. More than ever, perceptions of you are going to be formed based on your writing ability. You

---

15. http://www.writingcommission.org/report.html

may be a great coder, but if you can't express yourself in words, you won't be very effective on a distributed team.

The ability to write creates both a superficial perception of you and a real insight into how your mind works. If you can't organize your thoughts in your mother tongue so that others can clearly understand them, how can we expect that you can do it in a programming language? The ability to shape an idea and lead a reader through a thought process to a logical conclusion is not much different from the ability to create a clear design and system implementation that future maintainers will be able to understand.

This isn't all about being judged, either. If you have team members in different time zones and distant locations, writing may be the only way you have to explain what you've done, how you've designed something, or what your team members need to work on.

Communication, especially by means of writing, is the bottleneck through which all your wonderful ideas must pass. You *are* what you can *explain*.

> You *are* what you can *explain*.

Act on It!

1. Start keeping a development diary. Write a little in it each day, explaining what you've been working on, justifying your design decisions, and vetting tough technical or professional decisions. Even though you are the primary (or only—it's up to you) audience, pay attention to the quality of your writing and to your ability to clearly express yourself. Occasionally reread old entries, and critique them. Adjust your new entries based on what you liked and disliked about the old ones. Not only will your writing improve, but you can also use this diary as a way to strengthen your understanding of the decisions you make and as a place to refer to when you need to understand how or why you did something previously.

2. Learn to type. If you don't already "touch type," take a course or download some software that will teach you. You're more likely to be comfortable and natural in your writing if you are comfortable with the input method itself. Of course, with all this writing you'll be doing, you'll save yourself some time by learning to type quickly.

Being Present

You have the advantage of being face to face with your leaders and your business customers. Don't squander the opportunity.

While I was living in Bangalore as CTO of our software development center, I had the unpleasant experience of reporting to a manager who I not only disliked (and who disliked me) but who was in the United States. We had strained, late-night or early-morning phone conversations, made increasingly frustrating by background noise or unintended disconnections. I would write long, descriptive e-mails in an attempt to help close the distance and time zone gap, only to be ignored. And, if I complained about being ignored, I would be criticized for writing long e-mails. It seemed like a no-win situation.

My company at the time had an annual performance review process in which managers would list their employees' strengths and (so-called) development needs. The top of my development needs list that year was something called *presence*.

Now, presence in this context is an ultracorporate word describing an ever-so-fuzzy leadership trait. It's the unmeasurable quality of having your presence felt—particularly in face-to-face situations. It also includes the equally unmeasurable quality of carrying yourself like a leader.

When I was sitting down talking about my performance review (over the phone) with my beloved manager, I muted my phone when she said "presence." I didn't want the laugh to be audible. I wondered if she could hear the half-grimace and half-smile that I couldn't wipe from my lips for the rest of our conversation. She and I both knew that the *real* problem was presence in the more common form of the word: I just wasn't there in the United States with everyone else.

Most of us who were willing to share our feelings disliked this manager. She did little to command respect, so it wasn't much of a surprise. The pattern that emerged was that the only employees who had really *negative* relationships with her were the ones who weren't in the same geographic place as her.

Those in other countries such as India, Hungary, and Great Britain (in decreasing order) had strained relationships with her, since we were not only physically separated but we had time zone, infrastructure, culture, and language boundaries as well.

It seemed as though even for the people in the United States who were doing everything they could to avoid this manager, physical proximity and the occasional face-to-face conversation was all it took to make this manager comfortable. And, of course, the "out of sight, out of mind" phenomenon was very quickly validated when I hit the ground in India.

In addition to just telling a story about a bad manager, you can learn something from this experience. Physical proximity is an advantage in the workplace.

Think about the last time a relative or friend who was not computer savvy called you to ask for help with a computer problem. You try to walk them through the problem over the phone, and if they're not getting it, you just get more and more agitated. *If I could only just show them….* In contrast, face-to-face communication is incredibly effective. You can hear the other party more clearly. You can explicitly use visual aids to get points across by using hand motions or drawings on whiteboards. And, we all *implicitly* express a great deal of content in our facial expressions without even consciously realizing it.

Not only do we see greater productivity and enhanced communication from face-to-face interactions, but we also form tighter personal bonds. It takes a lot longer to create something you would call a friendship if you never meet someone in person. Fifteen years ago, it was unheard of. These days, with the ubiquity of the Internet, it's just less common than traditional face-to-face friendships. For many of the same reasons that we work less effectively via phone, e-mail, and chat, we are also much less efficient in building relationships that way. Add to that the discomfort of the unnaturalness of e-mail and chat-based conversation (something that the next generation probably won't remember), and in the majority of cases, the relationship built in a remote work environment will remain strictly centered around accomplishing tasks.

A strong team relationship with effective, high-bandwidth communication makes for better software delivered faster. In most business environments, important project decisions are made in person, over coffee breaks and in side conversations. These are fairly obvious observations, and the advantage one has by being a part of this is also fairly obvious. What's not so obvious—especially to us geeks—is the importance of being *seen*.

I *never* go into a bank. I do any banking I have to do either online or via automated teller machines. My grandparents are different. They do virtually all their banking *in the bank* talking to *real people*. They don't even like to do business over the phone. It just doesn't make them comfortable. They also know the people at the grocery store they go to. They go back over and over again and chat with them as they're checking out. They wouldn't consider changing grocery stores (or banks), because the choice of bank or grocery store is more than a pragmatic weighing of cost and convenience. It's personal.

Until we have robots or computer programs to perform our performance appraisals, all business will continue to be personal. We people like to interact with other people in person. Some of us, anyway.

The natural work mode of a computer person is to hole up in a cubicle or office, put on a pair of headphones, and get into "the zone" until it's time to eat. Douglas Coupland, in his book *Microserfs* [Cou96], tells the entertaining story of a team having to buy flat food to slide under the office door of a programmer on a mission. This kind of focused isolation has become part of the culture and folklore of the software industry.

Unfortunately, speaking for your career, this is bad for business. If you're locked up in an office, accessible only by phone (if you answer) or e-mail and perhaps even working all hours of the night and sleeping late as a result, there's no difference between you being onsite with your bosses and your customers and being offshore. You are missing a huge opportunity to become a *sticky* fixture in your company. Remember, you need to make it *personal*, and to do that you have to remember the natural human tendency to want to work with other humans—not voicemail, e-mail, or instant messaging but actual people.

Learn about your colleagues.

In today's distributed environment, you may find that although you're in the same country as the people you're working with, you're not in the same city or state. Regular trips for face-to-face meetings are great in these situations if they're practical for you and your company. But, the best thing you can do is pick up the phone and call your bosses and co-workers. Don't use speaker phones when you can help it, and don't rely on scheduled meetings. You need to try to simulate the kind of casual, coffee-break conversation that you might experience if you lived and worked in the same place, so budget time for (apparently) spontaneous conversations. On occasion, take the opportunity to make the conversation personal. Let "How are you today?" continue into "What do you generally do on the weekends?" Try to actually learn about the *people* you work with. Not only does it more firmly entrench you into your company, but it's a more enriching way to live.

Act on It!

1. One day in the next week, force yourself (within reason) not to send any e-mail. Every time you would normally send an e-mail, either call the person you would have sent it to on the phone or (better) walk to their office and speak to them in person.

2. Make a list of co-workers, bosses, and customers who you don't talk to enough. Put recurring appointments on your calendar to call and check in with them (either by phone or in person). Make the conversations short and meaningful. Use them to communicate something work related and also to simply make a human connection.

Suit Speak

My young nephews all use computers regularly. They are, relatively speaking, quite computer savvy. They use computers to communicate with friends all over the world. They are completely comfortable with instant messaging, e-mail, web browsing, and of course personal publishing and the other stuff you might use if you were a high-school student working on assignments.

But, if I were to brag to them that my new computer had a 10,000 RPM Serial ATA hard drive, they might at best do a teenage-level job of feigning enthusiasm. They would probably be equally unimpressed if I told them it had several gigabytes of RAM and a GPU that was faster than the CPUs in the systems I used just five years ago.

However, if I told them they could run the latest first-person shooter at full resolution without so much as a stutter in the game's visual appearance, they'd sit up and take notice.

Gigahertz and revolutions per minute aren't interesting to the average fourteen-year-old boy. Computer games are.

Businesspeople aren't that interested in gigahertz and RPMs either. They like it when their applications are fast, because they don't have to wait while on the phone with a customer or while trying to close out the books for the quarter. But, they don't care how many requests per second your new custom application server process can handle.

Market your accomplishments in the language of your business.

Businesses and those who run them are interested in business *results*. So, marketing your accomplishments in any language other than the language of the business is ineffective.

You wouldn't market a product to American audiences in German. A soft drink company wouldn't try to sell a drink to consumers based on the measured quantity of red dye #8 it contains. Common sense tells you that to sell a product to an audience, you have to speak to that audience in a language they can both understand and relate to.

As a software developer, that means framing your accomplishments in the context of the business you work for. Sure, you *got it done*, but what *was* it? Why did it matter? How was this so-called accomplishment not just a waste of company time?

My guess is that if you were to think about the past month's accomplishments, you might not be able to articulate just *why* they were useful tasks to do in the first place. Sure, you might have been told to do them, but what benefit did they deliver to the business?

At General Electric, there is an urban legend that former CEO Jack Welch used to enjoy getting on the elevator of one of the tall GE buildings with whatever random GE employee might have gotten on with him. He would then turn and ask the already-frightened underling, "What are you working on?" and then (here's where it might hurt) "What is the benefit of that?" The moral of the story was that you should always have your *elevator speech* ready, just in case.

What would you say if your CEO asked you the same question out of the blue? Even given a few minutes to prepare, would you be able to explain the business benefit of the tasks you are doing or the tasks you had recently done? Could you do it in words that a totally non-technical senior executive could not only understand but also *appreciate*?

Act on It!

1. Make a list of your recent accomplishments. Write the business benefit for each. If there are accomplishments on the list that you *can't* write a business benefit for, ask a manager or trusted acquaintance how they would frame the benefit.

2. Make your elevator speech, and memorize it.

Change the World

The worst thing anyone at work can ask about you is "What does he (or she) do?" Having to ask this question means that they don't know what you've *done*.

It's sad, but I don't know what most of the people I've worked with in big-company IT have done. People just don't think that way. They go to work, do their assigned thing, and go home. There's no lasting impact, other than the trail of code, documents, and e-mail they leave behind them.

That's what happens when you show up to work without a *mission*. You just sit around waiting to be told what to do. And, when you do what people tell you, the only people who know what you've done afterward are the ones who asked you to do it. That's fine if you want to work in retail sales or maybe even if you want to be an offshore programmer.

> Have a mission. Make sure people know it.

But if you want to be a software developer in a high-cost country, you need to come to work with a mission. You need to effect change but not change within yourself or your own work (that's a given). You need to effect visible change through your team, organization, or company.

The change can be small. You might be carrying the torch for unit testing, driving test practices into the hearts of the unwashed masses of your company's programmer pool. Or, it might be something bigger, like a radical new technology introduction that will lead to cheaper, better systems made faster.

You do these things because you are internally *driven* to do them. You can't stand back and watch the people in your company do things wrong. You know things could be better, and you *have* to change them.

Of course, if you're out to change the world, you're bound to make some people angry. That's OK as long as your intentions are right.

Don't be a jerk about it, but don't tiptoe around always playing it conservative either.

If you *do* end up ticking a few people off, you can at least take comfort in the fact that they won't ever ask "What does *he* (or *she*) do?"

If you don't know what your crusade is, you probably don't have one. If you're not already *actively* trying to make your mark, you're probably not making it.

Act on It!

1. Catalog the crusades you've personally witnessed in the workplace. Think of the people you've worked with who have behaved as if on a mission. Think of the most driven and effective people in the places where you've worked. What were *their* missions?

    Can you think of any such missions that were inappropriate? Where is the line between drive and zealotry? Have you seen people cross it?

Let Your Voice Be Heard

The ideas we've explored so far have been fairly conservative and focused on being recognized for the work you do in your workplace. If you want to be noticed, move up, or even stay employed with your current company, the topics we've touched on will be critical.

But, how boring!

The world is changing. If you want to write your ticket, you have to think bigger than the IT workers of yesteryear. While moving from level-23 programmer to level-24 programmer analyst might *really be* your short-term career goal, as a programmer today, you need to think beyond the next promotion or even your current place of employment.

Set your sights higher. Don't think of yourself as a programmer at a specific company—after all, it's not likely that you'll be at the same place forever—but as a participating member of an industry. You are a craftsperson or an artist. You have something to share beyond the expense-reporting application you're developing for your human resources department or the bugs you've got stacked up in your company's issue-tracking system.

Companies want to hire experts. While a résumé with a solid list of projects is a good way to demonstrate experience, nothing is better at a job interview than for the interviewer to have already heard of you. It's especially great if they've heard of you because they've read your articles or books or they've seen you speak at a conference. Wouldn't *you* want to hire the person who "wrote the book" on the technology or methodology you're attempting to deploy?

In my previous life as a professional saxophonist, I played a lot in the clubs in and around Memphis's Beale Street. As I began to adapt to the computer industry, I saw a lot of overlap between the way you have to get your name out in music and in the computer industry. As a musician trying to find work, the following properties were always true:

- (This one's the most important.) The best saxophonist doesn't always get the gig.

- Who you've played with is at least as important as how well you play; musicians are *cool by association*.

- Sometimes, the better musicians are overlooked for work because everyone assumes they won't be available or because they are too intimidated to ask.

- Music works via a network effect. If your social/music network terminates before reaching someone, it's not likely you'll ever be asked to perform with that person until an intermediary connection is made.

The computer industry is the same way. No objective system exists for rating and employing software developers. Being good is important, but it doesn't get you all the way there. Our industry, like the music industry, is a big, complex web of people connecting each other. The more places you are attached to the network, the better your chances of connecting with that perfect job or career break. Limiting yourself to the company you work for places serious limits on the number of connections you can form.

What better ways than publishing and public speaking are there for your name to be propagated and your voice to be heard? So, how do you go from Joe Schmoe programmer to published author and then to public speaker? Start on the Web.

First, read weblogs. Learn about weblog syndication, and get yourself set up with an aggregator. If you don't know what to read, think of a few of your favorite technical book authors and search the Web. You will probably find that they have a weblog. Subscribe to their feed and to the feeds of the people they link to. Over time, your list of feeds will grow as you read and find links to the weblogs other people have been writing.

Now open your own weblog. Many free services are available for hosting and driving a weblog. It's dead simple to do. Start by writing about (and linking to) the stories in your aggregator that you find interesting. As you write and link, you'll discover that the weblog universe is itself a social network—a microcosm of the career network you are starting to build. Your thoughts will eventually show up in the feed aggregators of others like you, who will write about and spread the ideas you've created.

The weblog is a training ground. Write on the Web as if you were writing a feature column for your favorite magazine. Practice the craft of writing. Your skill will increase, and your confidence will grow.

Your writings on the Web will also provide work examples that you can use in the next step. Now that you're writing in your own forum, you might as well take your writing to community websites, magazines, or even books. With a portfolio of your writing ability available on the Web, you'll have plenty of example material to include in an article or book proposal. Get yourself in print, and your network grows. More writing leads to more writing opportunities. And all of these lead to the opportunity to speak at conferences.

Just as we started easily with the Web in our writing endeavors, you can start your speaking career in your local developer group meetings. If you're a .NET person, prepare a presentation for your local Microsoft development group. If you're a Linux programmer, do a talk at your Linux users group. Practice makes perfect when it comes to speaking. Be sure to put a lot of thought into preparing for these talks. Don't take them lightly. Though you're speaking only to a small crowd in your home city, this is where you live and work. A job *really* well done will (eventually) not go unrewarded. You'll find that if you give it the right amount of attention locally, these small talks are no different from the big ones at major industry conferences. Those are obviously the next logical steps.

With all these ways to get your name and your voice out there, the most critical tip of all is to start sooner than you think you're ready. Most people undersell themselves. You *have* something to teach. You will never feel 100 percent ready, so you might as well start now.

Act on It!

1. If you don't already have a weblog, create one right now. Go to one of the many free weblog hosting sites, and set one up.

    Now create a new text file on your computer. In it, create a list of possible weblog topics. These are future articles you're going to write. Don't limit yourself to epic ideas. Shoot for ideas you can write about in ten to twenty minutes. Stop when the list is ten items long (unless you're inspired—keep going).

    Save the file but leave it open. If you reboot, reopen the file. You have three weeks. Each day, choose an item from the list and write an article. Don't think too hard about it. Just write it and publish it. In the articles, link to other weblogs with related articles. As you read the list to pick each day's topic, feel free to add ideas to it.

After the three weeks are over, pick your two favorite articles and submit them to user-moderated news sites such as Digg and Reddit. If you still have ideas on your list, keep writing.

Build Your Brand

Brand building has two parts: actually making your mark so that people will recognize it and then making sure that mark is associated with positive traits. Recognition and respect.

Today, when we see a swastika, we think of Hitler and Nazi Germany. From a brand-building perspective, that's very good for the Nazis. They accomplished the first half of brand building: awareness. But, those of us who are mentally healthy have an extremely negative association with all things related to the Holocaust. So, the Nazis ultimately failed miserably in the positive association department. In fact, Hitler stole the swastika from the Hindus, perpetrating the crime that all companies serious about their brands struggle to prevent. To the Hindus, who lay original claim to the swastika (or *swasti*), it is an auspicious symbol of well being. But, now throughout the West, this spiritual icon has been defamed. Lots of recognition and little respect.

On the flip side is Charlie Wood.[16] Charlie is an incredible singer, songwriter, and Hammond B3 organ player in Memphis, Tennessee. He plays five nights a week in a club on Beale Street. Everyone who knows him or has heard him knows how amazing he is. They all look up to him. He is as talented as you can get when it comes to rhythm and blues music.

But relatively nobody knows who the hell he is. No recognition and lots of respect.

What *you* want is both recognition and respect. Your name is your brand.

Your name is your brand. This entire part of the book is all about how to get both recognition and respect. Right here in this paragraph, what you need to understand is that the combination of the two is an asset worth building and guarding. Unlike a big, scared,

---

16. http://www.charliewood.us

corporate marketing department suing college kids over websites that misappropriate a corporate image or phrase, you don't need to spend too much time guarding your brand against *other* people. The most potentially destructive force for Brand You is yourself.

Don't water down what you stand for. Be careful where you let your name show up. Don't do lousy projects or send lousy e-mails to large groups of people (or make lousy weblog posts for the whole Internet to read). Don't be a jerk. Nobody likes a jerk, even if they somehow *deserve* to be a jerk.

Most important, remember that the things you choose to do and associate yourself with have a

Google never forgets.

lasting impact on what your name means to people. And, now that so many of our interactions take place via the Internet on public forums, websites, and mailing lists, a lot of our actions are public record and are cached, indexed, and searchable—forever.

You might forget, but Google doesn't.

Guard your brand with all your might. Protect it from yourself. It's all you've got.

Act on It!

1. *Google yourself*—Search Google for your full name in quotes. Look through the first four pages of results (are there actually four pages of results?). What could someone surmise about you following only the links from the first four pages of Google results? Are you even represented in the first four pages of search results for your name? Is the picture that these first four pages paints a picture that you appreciate?

    Do the same search again, but this time pay special attention to forum and mailing list conversations. Are you a jerk?

Release Your Code

Imagine how much easier it would be to find a job if there were companies already relying on software you had written. You could say, "Oh, are you running Nifty++? I can help you with that—I wrote it." That would be different. Interviewers and hiring managers would remember you. That's what you want.

Just a decade ago, while sounding like a wonderful idea, there wouldn't have been many opportunities for such a scenario to be played out. You would have had to work for a commercial software vendor first, and your credentials would have been tied to the products you helped develop while working for that software vendor. But things have changed. You don't have to work for the Big Guys to develop popular, name-brand software anymore.

Now there's another outlet: open source. Open source software has hit the mainstream. As IT shops start new projects, the age-old debate has shifted from *build vs.buy* to *build vs.buy vs. download*. If not entire applications, frameworks ranging from small libraries to full-blown application containers are being released under open source licenses and are becoming de facto standards.

And the people who are developing this software, for the most part, are people like you. They are people sitting in their homes in the evenings and on the weekends, pounding out software as a labor of love. Sure, there are some corporate-funded efforts creating or supporting open source products. But, the majority of open source developments are done by independent developers as a hobby.

> **Anyone can use Rails. Few can say Rails *contributor*.**

Although many of these contributing developers are just having fun and expressing themselves, some real incentives exist there. They are moving their way up the social chain of a community. They are building a name for themselves. They are building a reputation in the industry. They may not be doing it on purpose, but they are *marketing* themselves in the process.

Aside from building a name for yourself, contributing to open source software shows you are passionate about your field. Even if a company hasn't used or heard of your software, the fact that you've created and released it is a differentiator in itself. Think about it this way; if you were looking to hire someone as a software developer, would you prefer to pick someone who puts in their nine-to-five day and then goes home and watches TV? Or would you prefer someone who is so passionate about software development that they take it upon themselves to do software development after-hours and on weekends?

Open source contributions *demonstrate* skill. If you're making real code and contributing to a real project, it's a lot better on your résumé than just *saying* you know a technology. Anyone can write Rails or Nant on their résumé. Very few can write *Rails contributor* or *Nant committer*.

Leading an open source project can demonstrate much more than technical ability. It takes skills in leadership, release management, documentation, and product and community support to foster a community around your efforts. And, if you do *these* things successfully—in your spare time as a hobby—you'll be amazingly different from most of the other people competing for the same jobs. Most companies can't *pay* their developers to do all these things and do them well. Most can't even pay their developers to do *some* of them well. Showing that you not only can do them but you care enough to do them for free shows an incredible amount of initiative.

If you create something really useful, you might even end up being famous. You could be famous in a small technical field—maybe famous among Rails people, for example. Or if you're lucky, you could be *really* famous even outside the geek community like Linus Torvalds or...well, like Linus. Even if you're not quite famous, releasing your code will definitely make you *more* famous. If fame means that lots of people know who you are, then having one more person know about you makes you more famous. And the open source community is a *worldwide* network of people who, searching the Web for code, may come across your software, install it, and use it. In doing so, they will come to know about you, and as your software spreads, so will your name and reputation. That's what marketing is all about. That's what you want.

Act on It!

1. Stuart Halloway[17] does a workshop at conferences he calls "Refacto-tum." If you get a chance to participate, I highly recommend it, but the gist is as follows: Take a piece of open source software with unit tests. Run the unit tests through a code coverage analyzer. Find the least-tested part of the system and write tests to improve the coverage of that code. Untested code is often untestable code. Refactor to make the code more testable. Submit your change as a patch.

    The beautiful thing about this is it's measurable and can be done quickly. There's no excuse not to try it.

---

17. http://thinkrelevance.com

Remarkability

Traditional marketing curricula refer to the four p's of marketing: product, price, promotion, and placement. The idea is that if you cover all four of these categories, you'll have a complete marketing plan. Equal weighting is put on each of the four categories.

But, what is the goal of marketing? Its purpose is to create a connection between producers and consumers of a product or service. This link starts with awareness about a product. The traditional mechanism of building awareness is through promotions, including things like advertisements, mailings, and educational seminars.

Recently the marketing world has turned its attention to what is called *viral*—word of mouth—marketing. Viral marketing happens when an idea is remarkable enough that consumers spread it from one person to the next. It spreads like a virus, with each new infected consumer potentially infecting many others.

Viral marketing is preferred not simply because it's expensive to send out paper mailing and buy television ad space. It's preferred because consumers trust their friends more than they trust television commercials and junk mail. They are more likely to buy something they hear about from a colleague at work than something on a pamphlet they dig out from the middle of their Sunday newspaper.

In his book *Purple Cow: Transform Your Business by Being Remarkable* [God03], master marketer Seth Godin makes the somewhat obvious assertion that the best way to get a consumer to remark on a product is to make your product remarkable. Godin goes so far as to say that the traditional four p's are obsolete and that consumers have become numb to the old spray-and-pray strategies of mass marketing. The only way to stand out in the crowd, he says, is truly to be outstanding.

So, here's where the cynical readers start to applaud. All the marketing mumbo jumbo you might try is nothing compared to the power of a remarkable set of capabilities. Before you start saying "I told you so," we should probably talk about the definition of *remarkable*.

Remarkable definitely doesn't mean the same thing as good. Usually, products that are remarkable *are* good. But, products that are good are seldom remarkable. To be remarkable means that something is worthy of attention. You will not become a remarkable software developer by simply being better than all the other software developers you know. Being incrementally better than someone else isn't striking enough to result in the viral spread of your reputation. If someone were to ask, you might have a glowing report card, but *remarkability* means that people talk about you *before* they are asked.

To be remarkable, you have to be significantly different from those around you. Many of the self-marketing strategies discussed in this chapter are geared toward remarkability. Releasing successful open source software, writing books and articles, and speaking at conferences may all increase your remarkability.

Demo or die! If you look back at that last sentence, though not an exhaustive list, you'll notice that each of the items I've included as being potentially remarkable involve *doing something*. You might be the smartest or the fastest, but just *being* isn't good enough. You have to be *doing*.

Godin uses the phrase *purple cow* to remind us of what it takes to be remarkable. Not *best cow* or *most milk-giving cow* or *prettiest cow*. A *purple* cow would stand out in a crowd of best, most milk-giving, and prettiest cows. It would be the purple one that you would talk about if you saw that group.

What can you do that would make you and your accomplishments like the purple cow? Don't just master a subject—write the book on it. Write code generators that take what used to be a one-week process to a five-minute process. Instead of being respected among your co-workers, become your city's most recognized authority on whatever technologies you're focusing on by doing seminars and workshops. Do something previously unthinkable on your next project.

Don't let yourself *just* be the best in the bunch. Be the person and do the things that people can't *not* talk about.

Act on It!

1. Start small, but try to do *something* remarkable on your current project or job. One way to experiment is to shoot for remarkable productivity. Project schedules often have a lot of padding. Find

something that everyone thinks is going to take a week and do it in a day. Work extra hours for it if you need to do so. You don't have to make a habit of working extra hours, but this is an experiment. Do the work in a remarkably short time. See whether people "remark." If not, why not? If so, in what ways? Fine-tune the variables, and try again.

Making the Hang

When I was a young jazz saxophonist in Arkansas, people often asked me, "Oh, do you know Chris?" I didn't. Chris was apparently the *other* high-school teenager in Arkansas who was a serious aspiring jazz musician. So, when people met me, they would make the obvious connection, expecting us to be comrades in our very un-high-schoolish jazziness.

One summer, I had the opportunity to see the Count Basie Jazz Orchestra perform an outdoor concert at an amphitheater on the bank of the Arkansas River. Through some combination of good mood and uncharacteristic courage, I ended up backstage chatting with the musicians before they went on. I've never been a very chatty person, so this was a real twist of fate. I stood in the back talking to one of the saxophonists from the orchestra, and another young kid walked up and started chatting. After five or ten minutes, the band started, leaving the two of us standing unattended. "Are you Chris/Chad?" we said simultaneously.

In the years to come, I would spend a lot of my free time with Chris. Chris, I soon learned, had a strange knack for associating himself with the town's best musicians. He was just a high-school kid. But, he was already playing gigs, substituting for Little Rock's most respected jazz pianists. Chris was pretty good—especially for his age—but he wasn't *that* good.

It didn't take me long to understand what was happening. We went out, several nights per week sometimes, to clubs where jazz music was being performed. It was always a somewhat uncomfortable experience for introverted me, because like clockwork, when the band we were watching took a set break, Chris would break mid-sentence and just walk away from me to go talk to the band members. He was like a robot. I have to admit, it was a little sickening to watch him. He was so predictable. Wasn't he annoying these poor musicians? They were taking a break, for God's sake. They didn't want to talk to this damned kid! Being left hanging, I had to either follow him or sit awkwardly by myself waiting. Occasionally, on the days when I just didn't have the energy, I chose the latter. However, for the most part I would follow Chris and try to pretend I was fitting in.

Usually, much to my surprise, the musicians on break actually seemed to enjoy talking to Chris—and even to me. He was pushy as hell and would always ask if he could sit in with the band, no matter how inappropriate it seemed to me. He would also ask the musicians for lessons, which meant that he would go to their houses, listen to music, and chat about jazz improvisation with them. I would occasionally be dragged along, with the same feeling I had on the set breaks—that I was imposing.

But, I was obviously the one who was confused about this relationship that Chris was developing with these musicians. He was getting real, paying gigs with really good musicians. I was just some guy who hung around with him. He was my conduit to the city's best musicians. The only difference between us being that he was more outgoing.

Over the years, Chris's "be the worst" strategy coupled with the ability to unabashedly force himself on people, led him to become an incredible pianist. In fact, he squeezed his way into playing with some really famous jazz musicians. I, on the other hand, was still the guy he knew. He pulled me into some of these more high-profile gigs, but it was always him doing the pulling—not the other way around.

Since then, I've seen the same pattern in people I've met in classical music, the American Tibetan Buddhist community, software development, and even the confines of a single office. Chris called it "making the hang," which made it even more repulsive to me. But, the short story is this: the really good people won't mind if you want to know them. People like to be appreciated, and they like to talk about the topics they are passionate about. The fact that they are the professional or the guru or the leader or the renowned author doesn't change that they're human and like to interact with other humans.

Speaking for myself (and extrapolating from there), the most serious barrier between us mortals and the people we admire is our own fear.

Fear gets between us and the pros.

Associating with smart, well-connected people who can teach you things or help find you work is possibly the best way to improve yourself, but a lot of us are afraid to try. Being part of a tight-knit professional community is how musicians, artists, and other crafts-people have stayed strong and evolved their respective artforms for years. The gurus are the supernodes in the social and professional network. All it takes to make the connection is a little less humility.

Of course, you don't want to just randomly start babbling at these people. You'll obviously want to seek out the ones with which you have something in common. Perhaps you read an article that someone wrote that was influential. You could show them work you've done as a result and get their input. Or, maybe you've created a software interface to a system that someone created. That's a great and legitimate way to make the connection with someone.

Of course, you can make the hang online as well as in person. A lasting connection is a lasting connection. The heroes of the software world are globally distributed. The same is true in the music industry, though you can't take for granted that all musicians are connectable via e-mail. So, the music world tends to form local professional clumps, whereas software developers have the advantage of being able to easily reach each other no matter where we may be. This makes it easy to not only reach out to the gurus in your own city but to reach out to the gurus, period. Some of the most influential minds in software development are readily accessible via e-mail or even real-time chat.

The story that leads to me writing *this book* actually started with an e-mail about a Ruby library to one of its publishers followed by many conversations via online chat. Though I was timid about sending that original e-mail, apparently it didn't annoy Dave too much, and here you are reading my words. Thanks, Chris.

Act on It!

1. Pick one of your favorite pieces of software and e-mail its creator. Start by thanking him or her for the software. Then make a suggestion, ask a question, or make some other attempt at establishing a human connection with them. Solicit a response of some sort. If the software is free or open source, offer to help in some way.

2. Think of someone local to you whom you admire or would like to learn from. Look for a situation where you can see the person (a users' group meeting or speech are good possibilities), and go out of your way to start a conversation, even if it makes you uncomfortable—*especially* if it makes you uncomfortable.

Can't We Just....

by Stephen Akers

Anyone who has spent much time in the workplace knows that there is an ongoing struggle between information technology (IT) and the business (those not in IT). The root of this contention is almost always misunderstanding, miscommunication, and mismanaged expectations. These issues are underscored on an almost daily basis by the various canned phrases both groups use.

For IT, the most hated of these phrases is "Can't we just…." It usually goes something like this: Can't we just outsource this work? Can't we just add more developers to the project? Can't we just do what we did last time? Can't we just make the application faster? Can't we just create a new database?

The problem is when many people in IT hear this phrase they focus on the word *just*. It makes them feel as if the business considers their request to be obvious, trivial, and easily accomplished. Any failure to implement would therefore indicate that IT was incapable of completing the simplest of tasks and should probably be replaced.

As a result, a common response to these requests is often "no." IT wants to make sure the business realizes their proposal is not only complex and difficult to execute but is in fact a bad idea. Herein lies the struggle. Ultimately what happens is the business walks away feeling like IT always says no, while IT develops the impression that the business has no clue what it's doing.

That's exactly what I used to think. In my opinion, what the business really needed was someone on their team who knew what they were doing. That's why at one point in my career I decided to leave IT to go and join the business. I fully expected all my projects to be raging successes because I understand how to do things the right way.

It's funny how our plans don't always turn out the way we expect them to turn out. Although I did achieve success on the business team, it wasn't the kind of slam dunk I was looking forward to experiencing.

Can't We Just.... (continued)

Instead, I found out that I had a lot to learn myself. For example:

1. There are real commercial factors that act as constraints on nearly every project. These constraints will sometimes require you to implement the less than perfect technical solution.

2. Timelines proposed by the business are often not as arbitrary as they seem. Many times the delivery date of a solution can have a rippling effect on the success of the project or even on the company's performance.

Once I learned these lessons, I realized that IT has been focusing on the wrong part of "Can't we just...." The operative word in the phrase is actually *we*. This word implies that the business is reaching out to IT as a critical part of their team. They are reaching out to IT for help in putting together a solution that will result in success for the company.

So, the next time you hear that dreaded phrase, fight the urge to say "no." Focus on the word *we* and confidently say, "Yes, *we* can add more developers to the project, but that wouldn't be a good idea, and here's why...." But don't stop there. It isn't enough just to explain your position. You need to dig deeper to find out what commercial constraints the business is operating under. Over time this will build up your knowledge of the business domain and give you a better appreciation for the problems that need to be solved. Combining this understanding with your technical expertise will transform you from an enabler who always says "no" to a partner who the business can't live without.

Stephen Akers is vice president of information technology at Genscape, Inc.

Part V

Maintaining Your Edge

Do you remember a pop star named Tiffany (no last name) from the 1980s? She was in the top of the Top Forty and a constant sound on the radio back then. She enjoyed immense success, becoming for a short time a household name.

When was the last time (if ever) you heard anything about her? My guess is that you can't remember. I can't.

Tiffany had what it took to be a hit in the 80s—at least for a short time. Then the 90s came along, and Tiffany was way out of style. Apparently, if she tried, she didn't move fast enough to hold the affection—or even the attention—of her fans. When the tastes of the nation turned from bubble gum to grunge, Tiffany suddenly became obsolete.

The same thing can happen to you in your career. The process in this book is a loop that repeats until you retire. Research, invest, execute, market, repeat. Spending too much time inside any iteration of the loop puts you at risk of becoming suddenly obsolete.

It can creep up on you if you're not explicitly watching for it. And when it catches you off guard, it's too late. Tiffany probably had no idea the grunge thing was going to take off. She was putting all of her efforts into being a teenage, bubble-gum pop star, and by the time grunge music took over the Top Forty, she was irreversibly out of style.

This part will show you how to avoid becoming a one-hit wonder.

Already Obsolete

Many of us are drawn to the IT industry because things are always changing. It's an exciting and fresh work environment. There's always something new to learn. On the flip side, though, is the disheartening fact that our hard-earned investments in technology-related knowledge depreciate faster than a new Chevy. Today's hot new item is tomorrow's obsolete junk with a limited shelf life.

In *Leading the Revolution: How to Thrive in Turbulent Times by Making Innovation a Way of Life* [Ham02], Gary Hamel talks about how the

Your shiny new skills are already obsolete.

incumbent industry leaders in any given industry become complacent and, through their complacency, develop blind spots. The more successful your business, the more likely you are to grow comfortable with your business model, making you incredibly vulnerable to those who come along behind you with a radical idea—even a stupid one—that might make your wonderful, winning business model look like an old, worn-out sweater at a disco. The same can be said of technology choices. If you've mastered the Big One of any given time period, such as J2EE or .NET at the time this book was published, you may feel extremely comfortable. It's the profitable place to be, right? Every job website and newspaper classified section serves as an affirmation of your decision.

Beware. Success breeds hubris, which breeds complacency. A wave like J2EE might feel like it will never end. But, all waves either dissipate or meet the shore eventually. Too much comfort for too long might leave you defenseless, wondering what you'd do in a non-J2EE world.

That being said, folks have been pronouncing COBOL's death for decades. Every new incumbent is called "the COBOL of the 21st century," or some variation thereof. These days, the label is applied to Java. As much as I hate to touch, see, or be near COBOL code, to call Java the COBOL of the 21st century is quite a compliment. As much as some of us would love to see it go away, COBOL is here, and it has been working for a *long* time. COBOL programmers have been working with COBOL for an entire career. That's really saying something in this roller coaster of an industry. It's hard to say whether the same kind of investment would work in today's economy.

COBOL's story is the exception—not the rule. Few technologies provide such a lasting platform for employment. The message here isn't to run out and shed yourself of your mainstream knowledge. That would be irresponsible. I *will* say that the more mainstream your knowledge, the greater risk you have of being left in the technology stone age.

We've all heard the extrapolations of Moore's law that say that computing power doubles every eighteen months. Whether the numbers are exactly correct, it's easy to see that technology is still advancing at roughly the same rate as it was in 1965 when Intel's Gordon Moore made this assertion. And, with these advances in hardware horsepower come advances in what is possible to do with software.

Computing power *doubles*. With technology progressing so quickly, there is too much happening for any given person to keep up. Even if your skills are completely current, if you're not almost through the process of learning the Next Big Thing, it's almost too late. You can be ahead of the curve on the current wave and behind on the next. Timing becomes very important in an environment like this.

You have to start by realizing that even if you're on the bleeding edge of today's wave, you're already probably behind on the next one. Timing being everything, start thinking *ahead* with your study. What will be possible in two years that isn't possible now? What if disk space were so cheap it was practically free? What if processors were two times faster? What would we not have to worry about optimizing for? How might these advances change what's going to hit?

Yes, it's a bit of a gamble. But, it's a game that you will *definitely* lose if you don't play. The worst case is that you've learned something enriching that isn't directly applicable to your job in two years. So, you're still better off looking ahead and taking a gamble like this. The best case is that you remain ahead of the curve and can continue to be an expert in leading-edge technologies.

Looking ahead and being explicit about your skill development can mean the difference between being blind or visionary.

Act on It!

1. Carve out weekly time to investigate the bleeding edge. Make room for at least two hours each week in order to research new technologies and to start to develop skills in them. Do hands-on work with these new technologies. Build simple applications. Prototype the hard bits of your current-tech projects in new-tech versions to understand what the differences are and what the new technologies enable. Put this time on your schedule. Don't let yourself miss it.

You've Already Lost Your Job

The job you were hired to do no longer exists. You might still be drawing a paycheck. You might be adding value. You might even be making your employer ecstatically happy. But, you've already lost your job.

The one certain thing is that everything is changing. The economy is shifting. Jobs are moving offshore and back on. Businesses are trying to figure out how to adapt. Things have not reached a steady point in our industry. Our industry is like the awkward adolescent going through puberty. Awkward, ugly, and different year after year—day after day.

So, if you were hired to be a programmer, don't think of yourself as a programmer. Think of yourself as maybe not a programmer anymore. Keep doing your job, but don't get too comfortable. Don't try to settle into the *identity* of a programmer. Or a designer. Or a tester.

In fact, it's no longer safe (as if it ever were) to identify yourself too closely with the job you were hired to do. If your surroundings are changing and the context of your work is constantly moving, clinging to your job creates an unhealthy dissonance that infects your work. You may find yourself as the would-be programmer doing the job of a should-be project manager. And doing it poorly.

You are not your job. Back before you lost your job, you might have had plans. You might have imagined your progression through the company's ranks. You would do your time as a designer and take the architect role when your just reward was due. You could see the entire progression from architect to analyst to team leader up the management chain.

But, you've already lost your job, and your plans have changed. They're going to keep changing. Every day. It's good to have ambition, but don't buy too heavily into a long, imagined future. You can't afford to have tunnel vision with something too far off in the future. If you want to hit a moving target, you don't aim for the target itself. You aim for where the target is likely to go. The path from here to there is no longer a straight line. It's an arc at best but most probably a squiggle.

Act on It!

1. If you're a programmer, try a day or two of doing your job as if you were a tester or a project manager. What are the many roles that you might play from day to day that you have never explicitly considered? Make a list, and try them on for size. Spend a day on each. You might not even change your actual work output, but you'll see your work differently.

Path with No Destination

One of America's biggest problems is that it is a goal-oriented society. We're a nation of people who are always focused on the *outcome* of a process, whether it is the process of learning, one's career, or even a drive in the car. We're so centered on the outcome that we forget to look at the scenery.

If you think about it, the focus on outcomes is logically the reverse of what we should be spending our time on. You typically spend all your time *doing* things and little of your time actually reaching goals. For example, when you're developing software, the development process is where you spend all your time, not on the actual event of the finished software popping out of the end of the process.

This is true of your career as well. The real meat of your career is not the promotions and salary advances. It's the time you spend working toward those advances. Or, more important, it's the time you spend working *regardless* of the advances.

If this is the core of your work life—the actual work—then you've already arrived at your destination. The goal-oriented, destination-focused thinking that you usually do leads only from one goal to the next. It has no logical end. What most of us fail to realize is that *the path* is the end.

Returning to the software development example, it's easy to get wrapped up in the delivery of the code you are creating. Your customer needs a web application up, and you focus on finishing that application. But, a living application is never "done." One release leads to the next. Too much focus on the end product distracts us from the real deliverable: the sustainable development of a new entity.

Focus on doing, not on being done.

Focusing on the ending makes you forget to make the process good. And, bad processes create bad products. The product might meet its minimum requirements, but its insides will be ugly. You've optimized for the short-term end goal—not for the inevitable, ongoing future of the product's development.

Not only do bad processes make bad products, but bad products make bad processes. Once you have one of these products that is messy inside, your processes adapt around it. Your product's *broken windows* lead to broken windows in your process. It's a vicious cycle.

So, instead of constantly asking "Are we there yet? Are we there yet?" realize that the only healthy answer is "yes." It's how you traverse the path that's important—not the destination.

Act on It!

1. In his book *The Miracle of Mindfulness* [Han99], Thich Naht Hanh presents a suggestion: the next time you have to wash the dishes, don't wash them to get them done. Try to enjoy the experience of washing the dishes. Don't focus on finishing them. Focus on the act of washing them itself.

    Doing the dishes is a mundane task that almost nobody savors. Software developers have a lot of similar drudgery to get through in the average day, such as time tracking and expense reporting, for example. The next time you have to do a task like this, see whether you can find a way to focus on the task as you do it instead of anxiously rushing to finish it.

Make Yourself a Map

When you're in maintenance mode, it's easy to snap into a groove and just keep on being like you are. As a software developer, you know this is true from your experience with systems. If you maintain an application or a library that other developers use, it will sit stagnant in bug-fix mode (or worse) unless you have a solid feature road map. You might make the occasional enhancement because of user requests or your own needs, but the code will usually reach a steady state and change at an exponentially slower rate because you consider it done.

But a living application is never done unless it's on the road to retirement. The same is true of you and your career. Unless you're looking to exit the industry, you need a road map. If Microsoft had considered Windows 3.1 done, we'd all be using Macintoshes right now. If the Apache developers had considered their web server done when they reached 1.0, they might not be overwhelmingly leading the market right now.

Your personal product road map is what you use to tell whether you've moved. When you're going to the same office day in and day out, working on a lot of the same things, the scenery around you doesn't change. You need to throw out some markers that you can see in the distance, so you'll know that you've actually moved when you get to them. Your product "features" are these markers.

Unless you really lay it out and make a plan, you won't be able to see beyond the next blip on the horizon. In Chapters 2 and 3, you discovered how to be intentional about your choice of career path and how to invest in our professional selves. Though I focused on what seemed like a one-time choice of what to invest in, each choice should be part of a greater whole. Thinking of each new set of knowledge or capability as equivalent to a single feature in an application puts it in context really well. An application with one feature isn't much of an application.

What's more, an application with a bunch of features that aren't cohesive is going to confuse its users. *Is this an address book or a chat application? Is it a game or a web browser?* A personal product road map not only can help you stay on track, constantly evolving, but it can also show you the bigger picture of what you have to offer. It can show you that no single feature stands alone. Each new investment is part of a larger whole. Some work fabulously well together. Others require too much of a mental leap for potential employers. *Is he a system administrator or a graphic designer? Is she an application architect or a QA automation guru?*

Although it's definitely OK to learn diverse skills—it expands your thinking—it's also a good idea to think about the story your skillset tells. Without a road map, your story might look more like a Jack Kerouac novel than a cohesive set of logically related capabilities. Without a road map, you might even *actually* get lost.

Act on It!

1. Before mapping out where you want to go, it can be encouraging and informative to map out where you've *been*. Take some time to explicitly lay out the timeline of your career. Show where you started and what your skills and jobs were at each step. Notice where you made incremental improvements and where you seemed to make big leaps. Notice the average length of time it took to make a major advancement. Use this map as input as you look forward in your career. You can set more realistic goals for yourself if you have a clear image of your historical progress. Once you've created this historical map, keep it updated. It's a great way to reflect on your progress as you move toward your newly defined goals.

Watch the Market

You'd be a fool to invest your money in a volatile stock and then ignore it. Even if you've done a great deal of research and made an intentional choice about *what* to invest in, the market is uncertain. You can't just fire-and-forget when it comes to investments. Even if a stock's value is increasing now, that doesn't mean it isn't going to start tanking tomorrow.

You might also be missing an opportunity. You may find a really safe bet, yielding a 10 percent annual return. That sounds like a pretty good deal as long as the rest of the market isn't suddenly doing much better than 10 percent. Your workhorse investment of today, even if it continues to perform, may not be very impressive compared to what's possible tomorrow.

As the conditions of the market change, not paying attention could result in money lost or money that *could* have been earned missed.

The same holds true for your knowledge investments. Java is the conservative choice of today. What might change to make that not true anymore? How might you know if it changed?

What if, for example, Sun Microsystems started showing signs of going under? Sun has lost its position of dominance over recent years, and Java isn't an open standard. Though now open source, it is dictated and developed by Sun. At any point, a dying Sun might attempt to suddenly make its language and virtual machine into a last-minute profit center. It might fragment the Java language with incompatible changes, causing an industry-wide panic.

With your head in your monitor coding, you might not even hear about something like this until it was too late. You might find yourself on the job market with a suddenly less valuable skill. This is an unlikely hypothetical situation, but something like this could happen.

Even more likely is that, comfortable in your current job with your current set of skills, you might remain blissfully ignorant of the Next Big Thing as it rolls in. Ten years ago, you would have been surprised to find out just how big object-oriented languages with garbage collection would become. But, there were definitely signs if you were watching. Ten years from now, who knows what the Next Big Thing will be?

You have to keep your eyes and ears open. Watch the technology news, both the business side and the purely technical side, for developments that might cause a ripple. As Tim O'Reilly[18] of O'Reilly and Associates says, watch the *alpha geeks*. Alpha geeks are those super-nerds who are always on the bloodiest tip of the bleeding edge, at least in their hobby activities. Tim's assertion, which I have since observed in the wild, is that if you can find these people and see what they're into, you can get a glimpse of what's going to be big one or two years down the road. It's uncanny how well this works.

However you choose to do it, you need to be aware that in the technology sector, what's a good invest-

> **Watch the alpha geeks.**

ment today will eventually *not* be a good investment. And, in case you pay attention to the mood of the market, it might catch you by surprise. You don't want this kind of surprise.

Act on It!

1. Spend the next year trying to become one of the alpha geeks. Or at least *make the hang* with one.

---

18. http://tim.oreilly.com/

That Fat Man in the Mirror

I am, unfortunately, overweight. I have been for a long time. While living in India, though, I lost a *lot* of weight. Part of it was because of diet. Part of it was because of exercise. But, mostly it was from getting sick. After I came back to the United States, I slowly gained the weight back. It was a disappointing thing, which I reacted to by signing up for a gym and a fitness instructor. The weight started coming back off.

I've gone through several such fluctuations. What's fascinating about them is that I can't really tell when I'm gaining or losing weight. The only way I know is if someone tells me or my clothes suddenly stop fitting the same. My wife sees me every day, so she can't tell either, and, in the United States, people generally don't mention it when you *gain* weight. In India, they do.

I can't tell, because I see me too often. If you're constantly exposed to something, it's hard to see it changing unless change happens rapidly. If you sit and watch a flower bloom, it will take a long time to notice that anything has happened. However, if you leave and come back in two days, you'll see something very noticeably different from when you left.

You'll notice the same phenomenon with your career. Actually, you *won't* notice it. That's the problem. You might look at yourself in the metaphorical mirror each day and not see an ounce of change. You seem as well adjusted as before. You seem as competitive as before. Your skills seem to be as up-to-date as before.

Then, suddenly, one day your job (or your industry) doesn't fit you anymore. It's just uncomfortable at first, but you've already reached a critical point at which you have to either act quickly or go buy a new pair of (metaphorical) pants.

When it comes to fluctuations in body weight, you have a scale, so it's fairly easy to measure your progress (or lack thereof, in my case). There is unfortunately no such scale for measuring your marketability or your skill as a software developer. If there were, we could sit you on a scale and autogenerate your paychecks. Since we don't have that scale, you'll have to develop your own.

An easy way to measure your progress is to use a trusted third party. A mentor or a close colleague doesn't live in your head with you and can help give you a more objective look at where you stand. You might discuss your abilities as a software developer, project leader, communicator, team member, or any other facet of the total package that makes you who you are. At GE, there is a process called a 360-degree review, which formalizes this idea and encourages employees to seek feedback from peers, managers, and internal customers. Despite the corporate doublespeak nature of its name, the process is a great way to get a number of different perspectives of yourself as an employee.

The most important thing to ferret out as you go through a process like this (either alone or with help)

Developer, review thyself.

is where your blind spots are. You don't *have* to fix all of them. You just have to know where they are. Without being explicit about it, you'll be blind to your blind spots. That's when the bad things happen and take you by surprise. Bad things will happen, so it's best to know they're coming.

Even if you had a magic *value scale* that you could weigh yourself on, it would do you no good unless you used it. Schedule your reviews. You won't reflect unless you make the reflection time explicit. Saying "Don't forget to ask for feedback" isn't a strong enough message. If you have a calendar program that pops up reminders, make appointments for yourself for self-evaluation. First determine your measurement system, and then put it on the schedule. If it's not a built-in part of your work life, you won't do it.

If your company has such processes in place already, don't write them off as HR nonsense. Take them seriously, and *make* good come out of them. They may be implemented poorly where you work, but the motivation (at least what *used to be* the motivation) for them is right on.

Finally, when you have your system in place and you have scheduled time to make sure it gets fit in, *capture the results in writing*. Keep your evaluation somewhere handy. Review and revise it often. Tying the self-evaluation process to a physical artifact will make it concrete.

Don't let obsolescence creep up on you like a pair of tight-fitting pants.

Act on It!

1. Do a 360 review:

    - Make a list of trusted people who you feel comfortable asking for feedback. The list should preferably contain representatives from your peers, customers, and managers (and subordinates if you have any).

    - Make another list of about ten characteristics you believe are important measurements of you as a professional.

    - Convert this list to a questionnaire. On the questionnaire, ask for participants to rate you in terms of each characteristic. Also include the question "What should I have asked?"

    - Distribute the questionnaire to the list of people from the first step. Ask that your reviewers be constructively critical. What you need is honest feedback—not sugarcoating.

    When you get the completed answers back, read through all of them, and compile a list of actions you are going to take as a result. If you've asked the right questions of the right people, you *are* going to get some actionable items. Share the outcome of your questionnaire with your reviewers—not the answers but the resultant changes you plan to make. Be sure to thank them.

    Repeat this process occasionally.

2. Start keeping a journal. It could be a weblog, as we discussed in Tip 39, *Let Your Voice Be Heard*, on page 149, or a personal diary. Write about what you're working on, what you're learning, and your opinions about the industry.

    After you've been keeping the journal for some time, reread old entries. Do you still agree? Do they sound naive? How much have you changed?

The South Indian Monkey Trap

In *Zen and the Art of Motorcycle Maintenance: An Inquiry into Values* [Pir00], Robert Pirsig tells an enlightening story about how people in South India used to catch monkeys. I don't know whether it's true, but it teaches a useful lesson, so I'll paraphrase it.

The people of South India, having been pestered by monkeys over the years, developed an ingenious way of trapping them. They would dig a long, narrow hole in the ground and then use an equally long, slender object to widen the bottom of the hole. Then they would pour rice down into the wider portion at the bottom of the hole.

Monkeys like to eat. In fact, that's a large part of what makes them such pests. They'll jump onto cars or risk running through large groups of people to snatch food right out of your hand. People in South India are painfully aware of this. (Believe me, it's surprisingly unsettling to be standing serenely in a park and have a macaque come suddenly barreling through to snatch something from you.)

So, according to Pirsig, the monkeys would come along, discover the rice, and stretch their arms deep into the hole. Their hands would be at the bottom. They would greedily clutch as much of the rice as possible into their hands, making a fist in the process. Their fists would fit into the larger portion of the hole, but the rest of the narrow opening was too small for the monkeys to pull their fists through. They'd be stuck.

Of course, they could just let go of the food, and they'd be free.

But, monkeys place a high value on food. In fact, they place such a high value on food that they cannot force themselves to let go of it. They'll grip that rice until either it comes out of the ground or they die trying to pull it out. It was typically the latter that happened first.

Pirsig tells this story to illustrate a concept he calls *value rigidity*. Value rigidity is what happens when you believe in the value of something so strongly that you can no longer objectively question it. The monkeys valued the rice so highly that when forced to make the choice between the rice and captivity or death, they couldn't see that losing the rice was the right thing to do at the time. The story makes the monkeys seem really stupid, but most of us have our own equivalents to the rice.

If you were asked whether it was a good idea to help feed starving children in developing countries, you would probably say "yes" without even thinking about it. If someone tried to argue the point with you, you might think they were crazy. *This* is an example of value rigidity. You believe in this one thing so strongly that you can't imagine *not* believing it. Clearly, not all values that we hold rigidly are bad. For most people, religion (or lack thereof) is also a set of personal beliefs and values that are unfaltering.

But not all rigidly held values are good ones. Also, many times something that is good in one set of circumstances is not good in another.

> **Rigid values make you fragile.**

For example, it's easy to get hung up on technology choices. This is especially true when our technology of choice is the underdog. We love the technology so much and place such a high value on defending it as a choice for adoption that we see every opportunity as a battle worth fighting—even when we're advocating what is clearly the wrong choice. An example I encounter (and have probably been guilty of myself) is the overzealous Linux fan base. Many Linux users would put Linux on the desktop of every receptionist, office assistant, and corporate vice president with no regard for the fact that, in terms of usability, the toolset just doesn't compare to much of the commercial software that's available for a commercial operating system. You look foolish and make your customers unhappy when you give the right software to the wrong people.

It's hard to tell you're losing weight because you see yourself every day. Value rigidity works the same way. Since we live every day in our careers, it's easy to develop value rigidity in our career choices. We know what has worked, and we keep doing it. Or, maybe you've always wanted to be promoted into management, so you keep striving toward that goal, regardless of how much you like *just programming.*

It's also possible for your technology of choice to become obsolete, leaving you suddenly without a foundation to stand on. Like a frog in a slowly heating pot of water, you can suddenly find yourself in a bad situation. Many of us in the mid-1990s swore by Novell's NetWare platform when it came to providing file and print services in the enterprise. Novell was way ahead of its time with its directory services product, and those of us "in the know" were almost cocky in our criticism of competing technologies. Novell's product was enjoying a healthy majority in market share, and it was hard to imagine the tide turning.

No single event made it obvious that Novell was losing to Microsoft. Microsoft never made that magic Active Directory release that made us all say, "Wow! Drop NetWare!" But, Netware has slowly gone from bleeding-edge innovator to legacy technology. For many Net-Ware administrators, the water was boiling before they ever even realized the pot was warm.

Whether it is the direction your career is taking or the technologies you advocate and invest in, beware of monkey traps. Those originally intentional choices may become the last handful of rice you find yourself gripping prior to your career being clubbed to death.

Act on It!

1. *Find your monkey traps*—What are *your* rigid assumptions? What are those values that guide your daily actions without you even consciously knowing it?

   Make a table with two columns, "Career" and "Technology." Under each heading list the values that you hold unfalteringly true. For example, under "Career," what have you *always* known to be one of your strengths? Or your weaknesses? What is your career *goal* ("I want to be a CEO!")? What are the right ways to achieve your goal?

   In the "Technology" column, list what you most value about the technologies you choose to invest in. What are the most important attributes of a technology that should be considered when making a choice? How do you make a scalable system? What's the most productive environment in which to develop software? What are the best and worst platforms in general?

   When you have your list down and you feel like it's fairly complete, go one at a time through the list and mentally reverse each statement. What if the opposite of each assertion were true? Allow yourself to honestly challenge each assertion.

   This is a list of your vulnerabilities.

2. *Know your enemy*—Pick the technology you hate most, and do a project in it. Developers tend to stratify themselves into competing camps. The .NET people hate J2EE, and the J2EE people hate .NET. The UNIX people hate Windows, and the Windows people hate UNIX.

    Pick an easy project, and try to do a *great* application in the technology you hate. If you're a Java person, show those .NET folks how a *real* developer uses their platform! Best case, you'll learn that the technology you hate isn't all that bad and that it is in fact possible to develop good code with it. You'll also have a (granted, undeveloped) new skill that you might need to take advantage of in the future. Worst case, the exercise will be a practice session for you, and you'll have better fodder for your arguments.

Avoid Waterfall Career Planning

Back in the beginning of this millennium, an initially small rebellion formed in the software industry. A group of experts in software development started to realize that among them there was a trend forming in the way software projects were both failing and succeeding. In an industry environment in which more software projects were failing than succeeding, they believed that they had discovered a way to do better. The group called themselves the Agile Alliance.

The industry at the time had led itself to believe that the only way to develop software projects was to follow a top-down, heavily planned, rigorous process. Analysts would define requirements in large documents, and architects would create architectures that they would hand down to designers, who would create detailed designs. These designs would be passed to developers who would codify the designs in some sort of programming language. Finally, after months—sometimes years—of effort, the code would be integrated and delivered to a testing group, which would certify it for deployment.

Sometimes some variant of this process would work. If everyone knew every detail of what they needed at the beginning of a project, this kind of planning and rigor could deliver well-thought-out, quality-controlled software. But most of the time, people don't know every detail of what they want out of a big project. The larger and more complex a project is, the less likely it is possible to imagine every feature in detail well enough to create a specification. This kind of process is a *waterfall process*, and that term is almost universally equated with bad process these days.

So, as the members of the Agile Alliance realized, following a heavy process as most organizations were doing back then resulted in well-tested, thoroughly documented software, which was not what the software's users wanted. The rebellion was to create a family of agile methodologies. These were software development processes that were geared toward easy change. Less time was spent up front planning and designing. Software is malleable, so changing it *can* be cheap. The agile methodologies assumed change as a constant part of software development and adapted themselves to make it as cheap and easy as possible.

It all sounds obvious now. But back then, the adoption of agile processes was a source of conflict and debate. In theory, the idea of detailed planning and rigor sounds obviously right. But in practice, it does not work.

Early in my own conversion to agile methodologies (specifically Extreme Programming), I started to see everything through the lens of agile development. The forces and motivations at play turn out to be more general than just software development. Whenever I had a complex problem to solve, I would realize that an iterative, change-friendly approach to solving it was always less stressful and more effective for me.

Somehow, though, it took me a long time to realize that the most complex project I ever had to manage—the most stressful and most critical—was my career. I had designed my career up front like a software waterfall project. And the same problems that occurred in software projects were starting to happen to me and my career.

I was on track to be a successful corporate vice president or chief information officer. I was doing pretty well on this track. I had rapidly gone from newbie programmer to software architect to manager to director and could easily see myself continuing up the chain. But, successful as I had been, I started feeling like all I was doing was work I didn't like. In fact, the more successful I was, the less likely I was to be in a job I enjoyed.

What I was doing to myself was the same thing heavy processes did to their customers. I was doing an *excellent* job at delivering a career to myself that I *didn't want*.

It was unintuitive to me at first, but the solution to such a problem is to simply *change* your career. That can mean a lot of things. For me, it meant getting back into the deep technology that got me so excited about the information technology industry in the first place. For others I've known, it has meant moving from system administration to software development, moving from an unrelated field into computer programming, or even dropping the profession altogether and doing something else they love.

Just as in software development, the cost of change doesn't have to be high. Sure, it might be hard to go from software testing to being a lawyer. But changing your direction from management to programming, or vice versa, isn't hard. Nor is finding a new company to work for. Or moving to a different city.

And unlike, say, building a skyscraper, changing your career doesn't require throwing away everything you've already done. I spend my days programming in Ruby at the moment, but my experience as a manager or setting up an offshore development operation are constantly relevant and helpful in what I do. My employers and clients understand this and take advantage of it.

The important thing to realize is that change is not only possible in your career but *necessary*. As a software developer, you would never want to pour yourself into developing something your client doesn't want. Agile methodologies help prevent you from doing so. The same is true of your career. Set big goals, but make constant corrections along the way. Learn from the experience, and change the goals as you go. Ultimately, a happy customer is what we all want (especially when, as we plan our careers, we are our own customers)—not a completed requirement.

Better Than Yesterday

Fixing a bug is (usually) easy. Something is broken. You know it's broken, because someone reported it. If you can reproduce the bug, then fixing the bug means correcting whatever malfunction caused it and verifying that it is no longer reproducible. If only all problems were this simple!

Not every problem or challenge is quite so discrete, though. Most important challenges in life manifest themselves as large, insurmountable amorphous blobs of potential failure. This is true of software development, career management, and even lifestyle and health.

A complex and bug-riddled system needs to be overhauled. Your career is stagnating by the minute. You are steadily letting your sedentary computer-programming desk-bound lifestyle turn your body into mush. All of these problems are much bigger and harder to *just fix* than a bug. They're all complex, hard to measure, and comprised of many different small solutions—some of which will fail to work!

Because of this complexity, we easily become demotivated by the bigger issues and turn our attention instead to things that are easier to measure and easier to quickly fix. This is why we procrastinate. And the procrastination generates guilt, which makes us feel bad and therefore procrastinate some more.

As I mentioned in Tip 49, *That Fat Man in the Mirror*, on page 181, I've struggled with getting and staying in shape for as long as I can remember. Indeed, when you're miserably out of shape, "Just get in shape" isn't a concept you can even grasp much less do something concrete about. And to make it harder, if you do something toward improving it, you can't tell immediately or even after a week that anything has changed. In fact, you could spend *all day* working on getting in shape, and a week later you might have nothing at all to show for it.

This is the kind of demotivator that can jump right up and beat you into submission before you even get started.

I've recently been working on this very problem in earnest. Going to the gym almost daily, eating better—the works. But even when I'm getting with the program in a serious way, it's hard to see the results. As I was wallowing in my demotivation one recent evening, my friend Erik Kastner posted a message to the social messaging site, Twitter, with the following text:

```
Help me get my $%!^ in shape...ask me once a day: "Was today
better than yesterday?" (nutrition / exercise) - today: YES!
```

When I read this, I realized that it was the ticket to getting in shape. I recognized it from the big problems I have *successfully* solved in my life. The secret is to focus on making whatever it is you're trying to improve *better today than it was yesterday*. That's it. It's easy. And, as Erik was, it's possible to be enthusiastic about taking real, tangible steps toward a distant goal.

I've also recently been working on one of the most complex, ugliest Ruby on Rails applications I've ever seen. My company inherited it from another developer as a consulting project. There were a few key features that needed to be implemented and a slew of bugs and performance issues to correct. When we opened the hood to make these changes, we discovered an enormous mess. The company employing us was time- and cash-constrained, so we didn't have the luxury to start from scratch, even though this is the kind of code you throw away.

So, we trudged along making small fix after small fix, taking much longer to get each one finished than expected. When we started, it seemed like the monstrosity of the code base would never dissipate. Working on the application was tiring and joyless. But over time, the fixes have come faster, and the once-unacceptable performance of the application has improved. This is because we made the decision to make the code base better each day than it was the day before. That sometimes meant refactoring a long method into several smaller, well-named methods. Sometimes it meant removing inheritance hierarchies that never belonged in the object model. Sometimes it just meant fixing a long-broken unit test.

But since we've made these changes incrementally, they've come for "free." Refactoring one method is something you can do in the time you would normally spend getting another cup of coffee or chatting with a co-worker about the latest news. And making one small improvement is motivating. You can clearly see the difference in that *one thing* you've fixed as soon as the change is made.

You might not be able to see a noticeable difference in the *whole* with each incremental change, though. When you're trying to become more respected in your workplace or be healthier, the individual improvements you make each day often won't lead directly to tangible results. This is, as we saw before, the reason big goals like these become so demotivating. So, for most of the big, difficult goals you're striving for, it's important to think not about getting closer each day to the goal as it is to think about *doing better* in your efforts toward that goal than yesterday. I can't, for example, guarantee that I'll be less fat today than yesterday, but I *can* control whether I do more today to lose weight. And if I do, I have a right to feel good about what I've done. This consistent, measurable improvement in my *actions* frees me from the cycle of guilt and procrastination that most of us are ultimately defeated by when we try to do Big Important Things.

You also need to be happy with *small* amounts of "better." Writing one more test than you did yesterday is enough to get you closer to the goal of "being better about unit testing." If you're starting at zero, one additional test per day is a sustainable rate, and by the time you can no longer do better than yesterday, you'll find that you're now "better about unit testing" and you don't need to keep making the same improvements. If, on the other hand, you decided to go from zero to fifty tests on the first day of your improvement plan, the first day would be hard, and the second day probably wouldn't happen. So, make your improvements small and incremental but *daily*. Small improvements also decrease the cost of failure. If you miss a day, you have a new baseline for tomorrow.

One of the great things about this simple maxim is that it can apply to very tactical goals, such as finishing a project or cleaning up a piece of software, or it can apply to the very highest level goals you might have. How have you taken better action today for improving your career than you did yesterday? Make one more contact, submit a patch to an open source project, write a thoughtful post and publish it on your weblog. Help one more person on a technical forum in your area of expertise than you did yesterday. If every day you do a little better than yesterday toward improving yourself, you'll find that the otherwise ocean-sized proposition of building a remarkable career becomes more tractable.

Act on It!

1. Make a list of the difficult or complex improvements you'd like to make; they can be personal or professional. It's OK if you have a fairly long list. Now, for each item in the list, think about what you could do today to make yourself or that item better than yesterday. Tomorrow, look at the list again. Was yesterday better than the day before? How can you make today better? Do it again the next day. Put it on your calendar. Spend two minutes thinking about this each morning.

Go Independent

In stressful times, I often look back fondly at my days in a large corporation. I was nestled in both my own office or cubicle and a thick, fluffy, layered hierarchy of management. It was a joke to us then, but in a big company a smart person could get by with hardly getting *anything* done. In most cases, if a project didn't get done, there were enough people sharing the blame at enough layers that it was hard to figure out where things went wrong. And that's just for failures. If things took longer than they could have, the complexity of the organization obscured the reasons to a point that nobody really had a clue how long any project should take to get done.

So, on a day when you don't feel like really putting the pedal to the metal, a big company job affords you the opportunity to sit back and, say, browse the Web for a while. Or go home early. Or take a "sick day." For all I complained about big company life, it definitely had its perks.

The problem is that the safety blanket of corporate hierarchy slows you down. If you can hide behind the shield of mediocrity that most corporate divisions wield, there's not much incentive to excel. Even those of us who are generally well meaning are tempted by the restful oasis of YouTube or our favorite collection of web comics.[19]

In this way, a big company makes a wonderful place to go and semi-retire for a while if you're burned out. But if you're striving to be remarkable (which you are!), a big company is a hard place to find the right groove in the same way a bakery is a bad place to try to work off your love handles. The solution? Go independent!

You have a set of skills. You've honed them. You know what you're worth. Becoming an independent contractor is one of the ultimate tests. You have no bureaucracy to hide behind. You are directly accountable to the people paying the bills. The idea that you are providing a service becomes directly apparent in everything you do.

---

19. If you happen to be looking for one, try http://toothpastefordinner.com. I've giggled away many an hour there.

There is no team to share the blame when you do things wrong. It's only you, your expertise, and your ability to execute.

Becoming an independent contractor also forces you to learn how to market yourself and at the same time tests your choices in domain and technology to focus on. You can't rely on customers to find you when you go independent in the way that work will find you at a big company. You have to go out and *find* the customers. And once you've found them, you have to convince them that you're worth paying.

You also have to decide how much you're worth paying. Does what you do cost $50 per hour? Or does it cost $250? How will you pay your bills? How will you justify the money you think you're worth? *Are you really even worth as much as you thought you were?*

Going independent is hard. It puts all your skills as a professional to the test. You *might* not be ready for it yet. The good news is you don't have to go all the way. Consider it a personal development project, and put yourself in the market in your spare time. Set a goal to land a contract at a certain rate and finish it with a happy customer. Work on it at night or on the weekends (but please don't work on it in your cubicle at your day job!). You'll learn a lot without losing your safety net. Worst case, you'll overwork yourself for a few weeks, fail at one project, and be sent back to your comfortable cubicle with a new sense of appreciation for your job. The best case is that you are wildly successful, love the work, and set yourself on a new path toward career satisfaction and financial reward.

Reviewer Sammy Larbi suggests another alternative to going independent. If you currently work for a big company, consider joining a small one. If you work for an established company, try a startup. In a small startup, you can get the best of both worlds: a full-time job with a salary *and* the challenge of being pitted directly against the unfiltered problems of your business.

Curiosity Is a Strength

by Mike Clark

My parents will tell you I was an inquisitive kid. I asked lots of questions, read everything I could get my hands on, and learned how things worked by taking them apart. As it turns out, this wasn't just a phase—I never outgrew having an insatiable curiosity. It's easy to overlook, but I believe curiosity can be a strength. Sometimes it just takes a little practice to develop.

Looking back, I can identify several career-changing events that happened mostly because I followed a curiosity. I offer the following examples in hopes they encourage you to listen when curiosity calls:

I never figured I'd become a programmer. I'd always been fascinated with airplanes and spaceships, so enrolling in Embry-Riddle Aeronautical University's aerospace engineering program seemed like the logical choice. After a year or so grinding away, however, I discovered that the folks over in the computer science department were having a lot more fun. As part of a new degree program, they were applying computer science toward aviation-related problems. I had become curious about computers in high school but never really considered programming as a career. So, I started hanging out with the computer geeks to see what they were up to. Before long, I had switched degree programs. That single change ended up being one of my best decisions. The courses were still challenging, but I loved every minute. My initial curiosity in programming quickly became a passion that led me to apply for an internship at NASA and jump-started my software career. And to this day I never underestimate the potential reward of finding out what fellow geeks are working on for fun.

Whenever I get comfortable, I know it's time to try something new. After many years writing embedded software in the aerospace industry, I was comfortable (which for me is also associated with boredom) with C and C++. About this time, web programming piqued my curiosity, mostly because it was radically different from embedded systems programming. Unfortunately, the project at my day job didn't have web access (it was one of those super-secret projects), so instead I spent my nights and weekends learning how to write software for the Web. This hacking on the side eventually turned into an opportunity to work on a new project using Java. I ended up building web-based Java applications for many more projects...and employers. My curiosity about web development was the catalyst for diversifying my skills, which ended up being a good career move.

Curiosity Is a Strength (continued)

I learned Ruby and Rails on a whim. Ruby was a fun language that made me think about programming differently. Rails did the same for web applications. I didn't have any clients at the time who were paying for Ruby or Rails work, but that didn't really matter. I was curious, and I just couldn't help myself. I took a few less billable hours and spent that time digging into Ruby and Rails. Little did I know that in early 2005 I'd get an opportunity to build one of the first commercial Rails applications and get invited by Dave Thomas to help out on his Rails book. My curiosity about yet another new technology started another successful arc in my career.

I'm curious about more than just technology; business aspects are equally interesting to me. That led me to venture out on my own as an independent consultant and start a training company (The Pragmatic Studio). My curiosity about running a small business gave me the opportunity to learn a bunch of new skills: sales, marketing, customer support, and so on. Seeing the big picture has helped me become a better programmer.

So, what are *you* really curious about? Try following your interests for a little while and see what happens. You might be surprised where you end up!

Mike Clark is an independent consultant/programmer.

But I say to you that when you work you fulfill a part of earth's furthest dream, assigned to you when that dream was born, and in keeping yourself with labour, you are in truth loving life, and to love life through labour is to be intimate with life's inmost secret.

> *Kahlil Gibran, The Prophet*

Have Fun

If you've gotten to the point of being a software developer with the luxury to actually think about which direction you want your career to go in, congratulations! You can count yourself as very lucky. There are many cultures in which getting to decide what you do for a living is a great privilege which very few people enjoy. As a software developer, you're not likely worried about how to pay for a place to live or how to buy food.

You could have chosen any number of career paths, but this one is exciting. It's creative. It requires deep thinking and rewards you with a sense of being able to do something that most of the people you meet each day can't imagine being able to do. We may worry about progressing to the next level, making an impact, or gaining respect from our co-workers or our peers in the industry, but if you really stop to think about it, we've got it really good.

Software development is both challenging *and* rewarding. It's creative like an art-form, but (unlike art) it provides concrete, measurable value.

Software development is fun!

Ultimately, the most important thing I've learned over the journey that my career in software development has been is that it's not what you do for a living or what you *have* that's important. It's how you choose to accept these things. It's internal. Satisfaction, like our career choices, is something that should be sought after and *decided* upon *with intention*.

Resources

[Bec00]   Kent Beck. *Extreme Programming Explained: Embrace Change*. Addison-Wesley Longman, Reading, MA, 2000.

[Cou96]   Douglas Coupland. *Microserfs*. Regan Books, New York, NY, USA, 1996.

[DL99]   Tom Demarco and Timothy Lister. *Peopleware: Productive Projects and Teams*. Dorset House, New York, NY, USA, Second, 1999.

[GHJV95]   Erich Gamma, Richard Helm, Ralph Johnson, and John Vlissides. *Design Patterns: Elements of Reusable Object-Oriented Software*. Addison-Wesley, Reading, MA, 1995.

[God03]   Seth Godin. *Purple Cow: Transform Your Business by Being Remarkable*. Portfolio Hardcover, USA, 2003.

[HT00]   Andrew Hunt and David Thomas. *The Pragmatic Programmer: From Journeyman to Master*. Addison-Wesley, Reading, MA, 2000.

[Ham02]   Gary Hamel. *Leading the Revolution: How to Thrive in Turbulent Times by Making Innovation a Way of Life*. Plume, New York, NY, USA, 2002.

[Han99]   Thich Nhat Hanh. *The Miracle of Mindfulness*. Beacon Press, Boston, MA, 1999.

[Pir00]   Robert M. Pirsig. *Zen and the Art of Motorcycle Maintenance: An Inquiry into Values*. Perennial Classics, New York, NY, USA, Reprint Edition, 2000.

[Sil99]   Steven A. Silbiger. *The Ten-Day MBA: A Step-By-step Guide To Mastering The Skills Taught In America's Top Business Schools*. Harper Paperbacks, New York, NY, USA, 1999.

Be Agile

Don't just "do" agile; you want to *be* agile. We'll show you how.

The best agile book isn't a book: *Agile in a Flash* is a unique deck of index cards that fit neatly in your pocket. You can tape them to the wall. Spread them out on your project table. Get stains on them over lunch. These cards are meant to be used, not just read.

Jeff Langr and Tim Ottinger
(110 pages) ISBN: 9781934356715. $15
http://pragprog.com/titles/olag

You know the Agile and Lean development buzzwords, you've read the books. But when systems need a serious overhaul, you need to see how it works in real life, with real situations and people. *Lean from the Trenches* is all about actual practice. Every key point is illustrated with a photo or diagram, and anecdotes bring you inside the project as you discover why and how one organization modernized its workplace in record time.

Henrik Kniberg
(178 pages) ISBN: 9781934356852. $30
http://pragprog.com/titles/hklean

Refactor Your Career

Time to debug and refactor your career, and start doing it right. Start here.

Technical Blogging is the first book to specifically teach programmers, technical people, and technically-oriented entrepreneurs how to become successful bloggers. There is no magic to successful blogging; with this book you'll learn the techniques to attract and keep a large audience of loyal, regular readers and leverage this popularity to achieve your goals.

Paperback list price normally $33.00, now on sale for $9.95 while supplies last.

Antonio Cangiano
(288 pages) ISBN: 9781934356883. $33
http://pragprog.com/titles/actb

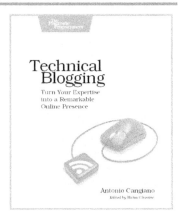

You're already a great coder, but awesome coding chops aren't always enough to get you through your toughest projects. You need these 50+ nuggets of wisdom. Veteran programmers: reinvigorate your passion for developing web applications. New programmers: here's the guidance you need to get started. With this book, you'll think about your job in new and enlightened ways.

This title is also available as an audio book.

Ka Wai Cheung
(160 pages) ISBN: 9781934356791. $29
http://pragprog.com/titles/kcdc

Think Better

Want to concentrate more effectively, and learn how to take advantage of your brain's wiring? We've got you covered.

Do you ever look at the clock and wonder where the day went? You spent all this time at work and didn't come close to getting everything done. Tomorrow, try something new. Use the Pomodoro Technique, originally developed by Francesco Cirillo, to work in focused sprints throughout the day. In *Pomodoro Technique Illustrated*, Staffan Nöteberg shows you how to organize your work to accomplish more in less time. There's no need for expensive software or fancy planners. You can get started with nothing more than a piece of paper, a pencil, and a kitchen timer.

This title is also available as an audio book.

Staffan Nöteberg
(144 pages) ISBN: 9781934356500.
$24.95
http://pragprog.com/titles/snfocus

Software development happens in your head. Not in an editor, IDE, or design tool. You're well educated on how to work with software and hardware, but what about *wetware*—our own brains? Learning new skills and new technology is critical to your career, and it's all in your head.

In this book by Andy Hunt, you'll learn how our brains are wired, and how to take advantage of your brain's architecture. You'll learn new tricks and tips to learn more, faster, and retain more of what you learn.

You need a pragmatic approach to thinking and learning. You need to *Refactor Your Wetware*.

Andy Hunt
(290 pages) ISBN: 9781934356050.
$34.95
http://pragprog.com/titles/ahptl

Lead Better

So you're the manager. Whether it's one project or a whole portfolio, learn what you need to do to make it work.

Paperback list price normally $34.95, now on sale for $9.95 while supplies last.

Johanna Rothman
(360 pages) ISBN: 9780978739249.
$34.95
http://pragprog.com/titles/jrpm

Too many projects? Want to organize them and evaluate them without getting buried under a mountain of statistics? This book will help you collect all your work, decide which projects you should do first, second—and *never*. You'll see how to tie your work to your organization's mission and show your board, your managers, and your staff what you can accomplish and when. You'll get a better view of the work you have, and learn how to make those difficult decisions, ensuring that all your strength is focused where it needs to be.

Johanna Rothman
(210 pages) ISBN: 9781934356296.
$32.95
http://pragprog.com/titles/jrport

Seven in Seven

Go beyond learning a new language, learn seven. And get up to speed on the latest NoSQL databases.

You should learn a programming language every year, as recommended by *The Pragmatic Programmer*. But if one per year is good, how about *Seven Languages in Seven Weeks*? In this book you'll get a hands-on tour of Clojure, Haskell, Io, Prolog, Scala, Erlang, and Ruby. Whether or not your favorite language is on that list, you'll broaden your perspective of programming by examining these languages side-by-side. You'll learn something new from each, and best of all, you'll learn how to learn a language quickly.

Bruce A. Tate
(330 pages) ISBN: 9781934356593.
$34.95
http://pragprog.com/titles/btlang

Data is getting bigger and more complex by the day, and so are your choices in handling it. From traditional RDBMS to newer NoSQL approaches, *Seven Databases in Seven Weeks* takes you on a tour of some of the hottest open source databases today. In the tradition of Bruce A. Tate's *Seven Languages in Seven Weeks*, this book goes beyond your basic tutorial to explore the essential concepts at the core of each technology.

Eric Redmond and Jim R. Wilson
(354 pages) ISBN: 9781934356920. $35
http://pragprog.com/titles/rwdata

The Pragmatic Bookshelf

The Pragmatic Bookshelf features books written by developers for developers. The titles continue the well-known Pragmatic Programmer style and continue to garner awards and rave reviews. As development gets more and more difficult, the Pragmatic Programmers will be there with more titles and products to help you stay on top of your game.

Visit Us Online

This Book's Home Page
http://pragprog.com/titles/cfcar2
Source code from this book, errata, and other resources. Come give us feedback, too!

Register for Updates
http://pragprog.com/updates
Be notified when updates and new books become available.

Join the Community
http://pragprog.com/community
Read our weblogs, join our online discussions, participate in our mailing list, interact with our wiki, and benefit from the experience of other Pragmatic Programmers.

New and Noteworthy
http://pragprog.com/news
Check out the latest pragmatic developments, new titles and other offerings.

Save on the eBook

Save on the eBook versions of this title. Owning the paper version of this book entitles you to purchase the electronic versions at a terrific discount.

PDFs are great for carrying around on your laptop—they are hyperlinked, have color, and are fully searchable. Most titles are also available for the iPhone and iPod touch, Amazon Kindle, and other popular e-book readers.

Buy now at *http://pragprog.com/coupon*

Contact Us

Online Orders:	*http://pragprog.com/catalog*
Customer Service:	*support@pragprog.com*
International Rights:	*translations@pragprog.com*
Academic Use:	*academic@pragprog.com*
Write for Us:	*http://pragprog.com/write-for-us*
Or Call:	+1 800-699-7764

CPSIA information can be obtained
at www.ICGtesting.com
Printed in the USA
BVHW04s0834020818
523280BV00004BA/62/P